LAUGHS, HOOTS & GIGGLES

LAUGHS, HOOTS & GIGGLES

By Joseph Rosenbloom

ILLUSTRATIONS BY JOYCE BEHR & SANFORD HOFFMAN

STERLING

New York / London
www.sterlingpublishing.com/kids

The material in this book in this book has been extracted from the following titles, all
published by Sterling Publishing Co., Inc.: *Wacky Insults & Terrible Jokes* Copyright ©
1983 by Joseph Rosenbloom; *Official Wild West Joke Book* Copyright © 1983 by Joseph
Rosenbloom; *Mad Scientist* Copyright © 1982 by Joseph Rosenbloom; *Looniest Limerick
Book in the World* Copyright © 1982 by Joseph Rosenbloom; *Snappy Put-Downs & Funny
Insults* Copyright © 1981 by Joseph Rosenbloom; *Monster Madness* Copyright © 1980 by
Joseph Rosenbloom; *How Do You Make an Elephant Laugh?* Copyright © 1979 by Joseph
Rosenbloom; *Silly Verse (and Even Worse)* Copyright © 1978 by Joseph Rosenbloom;
Gigantic Joke Book Copyright © 1978 by Joseph Rosenbloom; *Dr. Knock-Knock's Official
Knock-Knock Dictionary* Copyright © 1976 by Joseph Rosenbloom; *Biggest Riddle Book in
the World* Copyright © 1976 by Joseph Rosenbloom.

Library of Congress Cataloging-in-Publication Data Available

10 9 8 7 6 5 4 3 2 1

Published by Sterling Publishing Co., Inc.
387 Park Avenue South, New York, NY 10016
© 2007 by Joseph Rosenbloom
This is an abridged edition of *Laughs, Hoots, and Giggles*
originally published in 1984 by Sterling Publishing Co., Inc.
Distributed in Canada by Sterling Publishing
c/o Canadian Manda Group, 165 Dufferin Street
Toronto, Ontario, Canada M6K 3H6
Distributed in the United Kingdom by GMC Distribution Services
Castle Place, 166 High Street, Lewes, East Sussex, England BN7 1XU
Distributed in Australia by Capricorn Link (Australia) Pty. Ltd.
P.O. Box 704, Windsor, NSW 2756, Australia

Sterling ISBN-13: 978-1-4027-5063-2
        ISBN-10: 1-4027-5063-3

For information about custom editions, special sales, premium and
corporate purchases, please contact Sterling Special Sales Department
at 800-805-5489 or specialsales@sterlingpublishing.com.

CONTENTS

Jokes

Worse Verse

Grab Bag

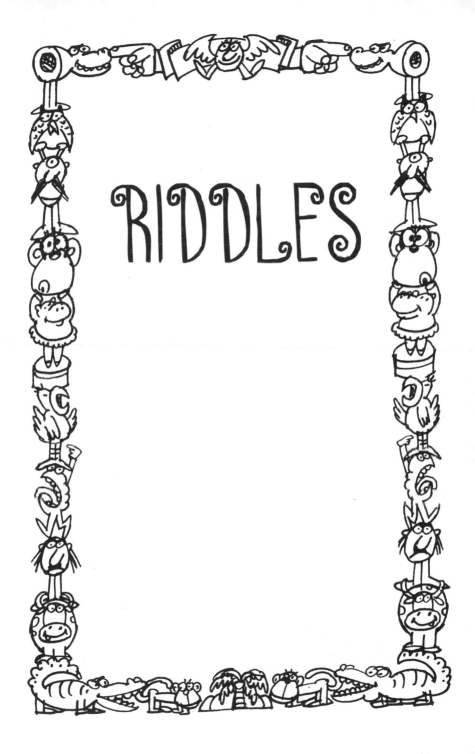

RIDDLES

Warm-Ups

What happens when you throw a
green rock into the Red Sea?

It gets wet.

What does an envelope
say when you lick it?

Nothing. It just shuts up.

Why shouldn't you tell a secret to a pig?

Because he is a squealer.

Where do frogs sit?

On toadstools.

Why should you leave your watch
home when you take an airplane?

Because time flies anyway.

If a man was born in Greece, raised in Spain, came to America, and died in San Francisco, what is he?

Dead.

How can you tell twin witches apart?

It's not easy to tell which witch is which.

What weighs more, a pound of lead or a pound of feathers?

They weigh the same.

Why did the man have to fix the horn of his car?

Because it didn't give a hoot.

Why did the nutty kid throw a bucket of water out of the window?

He wanted to make a big splash.

Why did the nutty kid throw butter out of the window?

He wanted to see a butterfly.

Why did the nutty kid throw a
glass of water out of the window?

He wanted to see a waterfall.

What paper makes you itch?

Scratch paper.

What can you break
without touching it?

Your promise.

Why do people always say to you,
"A penny for your thoughts?"

Because that's all they're worth.

A man was driving a black truck. His lights
weren't on. The moon wasn't out. A woman was
crossing the street. How did the man see her?

It was a bright, sunny day.

What doesn't get any wetter no
matter how much it rains?

The ocean.

What animal makes the most of its food?

The giraffe. It makes a little go a long way.

What insect gets high marks in language class?

The spelling bee.

When a dirty kid has finished
taking a bath, what is still dirty?

The bathtub.

What kind of bath can you take without water?

A sun bath.

What time is the same spelled
backward or forward?

Noon.

What do you get if you cross
an insect and a rabbit?

Bugs Bunny.

Why can't you read a
story about a bed?

It hasn't been made up yet.

Why did the kid avoid the cemetery?

He didn't want to be caught dead there.

What did the bee
say to the flower?

"Hello, honey!"

What did the fly say to the flypaper?

"I'm stuck on you."

What did the tree say to the woodpecker?

"You bore me."

Why did the kid put his
clock in the oven?

He wanted to have a hot time.

What ten-letter word starts with g-a-s?

Automobile.

What's drawn by everyone without pen or pencil?

Breath.

What goes around a yard but doesn't move?

A fence.

Why does a mother carry her baby?

The baby can't carry the mother.

What's a calf after it's six months old?

Seven months old.

What asks no question but demands an answer?

A doorbell or a ringing telephone.

What kind of apple has a short temper?

A crab apple.

How does a boat show affection?

It hugs the shore.

What kind of watch is best for people
who don't like time on their hands?

A pocket watch.

What goes up and down
but doesn't move?

A staircase.

What always comes into a
house through the keyhole?

A key.

What word if pronounced right is wrong
but if pronounced wrong is right?

Wrong.

What song does a car radio play?

A cartoon.

What has four legs and a back but no body?

A chair.

When does a chair dislike you?

When it can't bear you.

How did the man feel when he got a big bill from the electric company?

Shocked.

What did the man do when he got a big gas bill?

Exploded.

What did the man say when he got a big phone bill?

"Talk isn't cheap."

What's the best day to go to the beach?

Sunday.

What kind of bulbs don't need water?

Light bulbs.

Why is a fish like a person who talks too much?

Because it doesn't know when to keep its mouth shut.

How can you tell the difference between a can of chicken soup and a can of tomato soup?

Read the label.

What trees come in twos?

Pear trees.

What insect runs away from everything?

A flea.

What kind of cup doesn't hold water?

A cupcake.

What animal doesn't believe anything?

Sheep. They always say, "Bah!"

Why did the reporter put a flashlight into his mouth?

He wanted to get the inside story.

What's the first thing you see when you understand something?

The light.

Do you say, "Nine and five is thirteen," or "Nine and five are thirteen"?

Neither. Nine plus five equals fourteen.

What people travel the most?

Romans.

What person is always in a hurry?

A Russian.

What does Brazil produce that
no other country produces?

Brazilians.

What people are like
the end of a book?

The Finnish.

Who never gets his hair wet in the shower?

A bald man.

Why did Jack and Jill roll down the hill?

It beat walking.

How many animals did Moses take on the ark?

*Moses didn't take anything
on the ark. Noah did!*

What two things can't you have for breakfast?

Lunch and dinner.

What flower does everyone have?

Tulips.

What bird can lift the most?

A crane.

What belongs to you, but is used more by others?

Your name.

What did one wall say to the other?

"I'll meet you at the corner."

Why do firemen wear red suspenders?

To keep their pants up.

What's the difference between a pear and a pearl?

The letter L.

What does a caterpillar do on New Year's Day?

Turns over a new leaf.

What kind of coach has no wheels?

A football coach.

How do pigs write?

With pigpens.

What kind of tree do you find in the kitchen?

A pantry.

Where did the knights study?

In knight school.

What can run but can't walk?

Water.

What's the first thing you
do in the morning?

You wake up.

What's a zebra?

A horse with Venetian blinds.

How is an engaged woman like a telephone?

They both have rings.

Why do postmen carry letters?

*Because the letters can't go
anywhere by themselves.*

What kind of
hogs do you find
on highways?

Road hogs.

Who always goes to bed with shoes on?

A horse.

How is a toupee like a secret?

Because you keep it under your hat.

Spell "pound" in two letters.

Lb.

Why shouldn't you put grease on your
hair the night before a test?

If you did, everything might slip your mind.

What's the first thing you put into a room?

Your feet.

What's a sound sleeper?

Someone who snores.

If six children and two dogs
were under an umbrella,
how come none
of them got wet?

*It wasn't
raining.*

What kind of star wears sunglasses?

A movie star.

What's the difference between here and there?

The letter T.

Can you read the following?
Yy u r yy u b
I c u r yy 4 me.

Too wise you are, too wise you be,
I see you are too wise for me.

What did one math book say to the other?

"Boy, do I have problems!"

What piece of wood is like a king?

A ruler.

What do people make that you can't see?

Noise.

What did the squirrel say to his girlfriend?

"I'm nuts about you."

What did the girl squirrel answer back?

"You're nuts so bad yourself."

What did one candle say
to the other candle?

"Going out tonight?"

What kind of table has no legs?

A multiplication table.

On what kind of ships
do students study?

Scholarships.

When prices are going up, what
remains stationery?

Writing paper and envelopes.

What did one car muffler say
to the other car muffler?

"Am I exhausted!"

What did the big watch hand say
to the little watch hand?

"Don't go away, I'll be back in an hour."

What did the father tree say to his son?

"You're a chip off the old block."

What has teeth but no mouth?

A comb or a saw.

Where can you always
find money?

In the dictionary.

If cows talked all at once, what would they say?

Nothing. Cows can't talk.

Winners & Losers

How do chickens start a race?

From scratch.

What's a fast duck?

A quick quack.

Why did the orange stop in the
middle of the road?

It ran out of juice.

A lemon and an orange were on
a high diving board. The orange
jumped off. Why didn't the lemon?

Because it was yellow.

If you're swimming in the ocean and an
alligator attacks you, what should you do?

*Nothing. There are no
alligators in the ocean.*

Why shouldn't you tell a joke
while you're ice skating?

Because the ice might crack up.

Why don't sheep have much money?

They're always getting fleeced.

Why did the kangaroo
mother scold her child?

For eating crackers in bed.

What did the bee say to the rose?

"Hi, Bud!"

What did the rose answer?

"Buzz off!"

What did one grape say to the other?

*"If it weren't for you, we
wouldn't be in this jam."*

How is someone who borrows money but
doesn't pay it all back like a football player?

> *Because sometimes he gives you a quarter
> back and sometimes a half back.*

Two baseball teams played a
game. One team won but no man
touched base. How could that be?

> *Both were all-women teams.*

Why was Cinderella thrown
off the baseball team?

> *Because she ran
> away from the ball.*

What team cries when it loses?

> *A bawl club.*

Two men were playing checkers. They played
five games, and each man won the same
number of games. How is that possible?

> *They played different people.*

When it rains cats and dogs,
what do you step into?

> *Poodles.*

What did the frankfurter say
when the dog bit him?

"It's a dog-eat-dog world."

How is a ghost child taught to count to five?

One, boo, three, four, five.

What did the yacht
say to the dock?

"Yacht's up, Doc?"

What did the pitcher say to the cup?

"I'll have none of your lip."

When is it bad luck to have
a black cat follow you?

When you're a mouse.

What do you get if your sheep studies karate?

A lamb chop.

How do fireflies start a race?

When someone says,
"Ready, set, glow!"

What's the best way to win a race?

Run faster than anybody else.

Why do you run faster
when you have a cold?

You have a running nose.

If George Washington were alive
today, why couldn't he throw a silver
dollar across the Potomac?

Because a dollar doesn't go
as far as it used to.

What kind of sandwich speaks for itself?

A tongue sandwich.

How is an airline pilot
like a football star?

They both make
safe touchdowns.

Who are the happiest people
at the football game?

The cheerleaders.

What color is a cheerleader?

Yeller.

If your watch is broken, why can't you go fishing?

Because you don't have the time.

What's the best way to
communicate with a fish?

Drop him a line.

What did one fish say to the other?

*"If you keep your big mouth
shut, you won't get caught."*

What famous prize do cats win?

The A-cat-emy Award.

What dog has money?

*A bloodhound, because he is
always picking up scents.*

Why are dogs experts on trees?

*They have to be if they don't
want to bark up the wrong one.*

If you're crazy about chess, why should
you keep away from squirrels?

Because squirrels eat chestnuts.

What's the best advice to give a young baseball player?

If you don't succeed at first, try second base.

Which takes longer to run: from first to second base or from second to third base?

From second to third base, because there's a shortstop in the middle.

Where does Superman get the kind of food he needs to make him strong?

At the supermarket.

Why did the team sign a two-headed baseball player?

To play the double-headers.

A dog was tied to a 15-foot rope, but he walked 30 feet. Why?

The rope wasn't tied to anything.

What did the dog say when it was scratched by the cat?

Nothing. Dogs can't talk.

Why did the rooster refuse to fight?

Because he was chicken.

Why are mountain climbers curious?

They always want to take another peak.

What's a stupid mummy?

A dummy mummy.

Why did the mummy leave his
tomb after 2,000 years?

*He thought he was old
enough to leave home.*

Which burns longer, the candles on a boy's
birthday cake, or the candles on a girl's?

Neither. They all burn shorter.

When do turkeys eat nothing?

When they're stuffed.

Why were the elephants the last
animals to leave Noah's Ark?

They had to pack their trunks.

What's a sorcerer who
casts only good spells?

A charming fellow.

Why shouldn't you listen to people who've just come out of the swimming pool?

Because they're all wet.

When can you jump over three men without getting up?

In a game of checkers.

What kind of bell doesn't ring?

A dumbbell.

August was the name of a puppy who was always picking on larger animals. One day he got into an argument with a lion. The next day was the first day of September. Why?

Because that was the last of August.

Why do ducks look so sad?

When they preen their feathers, they get down in the mouth.

What kind of police officer dresses poorly?

A plainclothes officer.

Why are birds poor?

Because money doesn't grow on trees.

What drives a baseball batter crazy?

A pitcher who throws screwballs.

Why is a scrambled egg like a losing ball team?

Because both are beaten.

Why was the mummy sent into
the game as a pinch hitter?

*With a mummy at bat, the game
would be all wrapped up.*

Why did the silly couple want to
get married in the bathtub?

They wanted a double-ring ceremony.

Why couldn't the dog catch his tail?

*It's hard to make ends
meet these days.*

Why aren't horses well-dressed?

Because they wear shoes but no socks.

Why didn't horses like Theodore Roosevelt?

Because he was a rough rider.

What's the best exercise
for losing weight?

*Pushing yourself
away from the table.*

What do ants use for hula hoops?

Cheerios.

What kind of
insect likes
to bowl?

*A boll
weevil.*

Why do good bowlers play so slowly?

They have time to spare.

Why was the skeleton a coward?

He had no guts.

Why do skeletons
drink a lot of milk?

*It's good for
the bones.*

Why did the invisible couple
understand each other so well?

They could see right through each other.

What did the bow tie say to the boy?

"You double-crossed me."

What did the stove say to the pot?

"I can make things hot for you."

What did the window say
to the Venetian blind?

*"If it weren't for you, it would
be curtains for me."*

How can you make a slow horse fast?

Don't give him any food.

What did one horse say to the other?

*"I forget your name but your
pace is familiar."*

Women don't have it and don't want it. Men get it, think it's a good thing, but often get rid of it. What is it?

A beard.

What insect lives on nothing?

A moth, because it eats holes.

Why did the bald man put a rabbit on his head?

Because he wanted a head of hare.

Why was Adam known to be a good runner?

He was first in the human race.

If two people raced with sand in their shoes, who would win?

The one with the quicksand.

A cabbage, a faucet, and a tomato had a race. How did it go?

The cabbage was ahead, the faucet was running, and the tomato tried to ketchup.

What's the proper way to address
the king of the ghosts?

"Your ghostliness."

Why couldn't the mountain climber call for help?

Because he was hanging by his teeth.

Why are owls brave?

*Because they
don't give a hoot
about anything.*

What happened to the sardine
when it didn't show up for work?

It got canned.

3

World Records

What's the biggest ant?

An elephant.

What's the biggest building?

The library. It has the most stories.

Which American had the biggest family?

George Washington, because he was father of his country.

When the biggest elephant in the world fell into a 30-foot well, how did it get out?

Wet.

What's as big as an elephant but doesn't weigh anything?

An elephant's shadow.

What's the best way to
catch an elephant?

*Act like a nut and he'll
follow you anywhere.*

Who was the biggest thief in history?

Atlas, because he held up the whole world.

What's the best way to hold a bat?

By the wings.

How can you spell too
much with two letters?

XS.

When does a mouse weigh as
much as an elephant?

When the scale is broken.

What word grows smaller when
you add two letters to it?

Add "er" to short and it becomes shorter.

What's smaller than
an ant's mouth?

An ant's dinner.

What's a very small frankfurter?

An itsy bitsy, teeny wienie.

What's the longest word in the English language?

"Smiles," because there's a "mile" between the first and last letters.

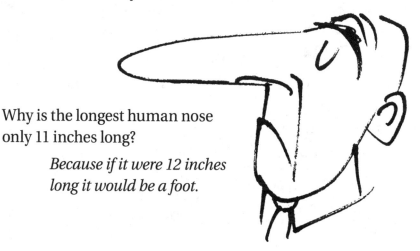

Why is the longest human nose only 11 inches long?

Because if it were 12 inches long it would be a foot.

What's the longest view in the world?

Down a road with telephone poles, because then you can see from pole to pole.

What kind of clothing wears the longest?

Underwear, because it's never worn out.

What's the shortest month?

May. It has only three letters.

What kind of pine has the sharpest needles?

A porcupine.

What flower is happiest?

A gladiolus.

What's the hottest day of the week?

Friday.

What's the hottest part of a man's face?

His sideburns.

When was beef at its highest?

When the cow jumped over the moon.

What fish has the lowest voice?

A bass.

What person adds best in hot weather?

A summer.

What's the laziest mountain
in the world?

Mt. Everest.

What's the poorest plant?

A vine, because it can't support itself.

What birds are noisiest?

Whooping cranes.

What person has the loudest voice?

The ice cream man.

What's the smartest animal?

A skunk, because it makes a lot of scents.

Which is faster, hot or cold?

Hot, because you can catch cold.

What animal grows the fastest?

A kangaroo. It grows by leaps and bounds.

What was the greatest invention in history?

The wheel, because it got everything rolling.

What kind of house weighs the least?

A lighthouse.

Who was the strongest man in the Bible?

Jonah. Even the whale couldn't keep him down.

Why did the farmer think he was the strongest man in the world?

Because he raised a 600-pound pig.

What's the strongest animal?

The snail, because it carries its house on its back.

Who has the strongest fingers in the world?

A miser, because he is always pinching pennies.

What's the most important subject a witch learns in school?

Spelling.

Who is the most musical grandfather you could have?

One who fiddles with his beard.

Where can you find the largest diamond in the world?

On a baseball field.

What's the biggest baseball team?

The Giants.

In what part of a ballpark do you
find the whitest clothes?

In the bleachers.

What are the best stockings for
baseball players to wear?

Stockings with runs in them.

Where are the headquarters for
the Umpire's Association?

The Umpire State Building.

What's the quietest sport?

Bowling, because you can hear a pin drop.

What's the loudest sport?

Tennis, because everyone raises a racket.

What's the hardest thing about
learning to roller skate?

The ground.

What's the easiest way to make a banana split?
Cut it in half.

When is a boat cheapest?
When it's a sail boat.

What's the easiest
way to grow tall?
Sleep long.

What's more invisible than an invisible man?
The shadow of an invisible man.

What's the best thing to put into a pie?
Your teeth.

What's the best key to have?
Lucky.

How did the 800-pound man feel
when he lost 250 pounds?

Delighted.

An elephant always remembers, but
what kind of animal always forgets?

*An owl, because it keeps
saying, "Who? Who?"*

What dog doesn't bark no
matter what you do to him?

A hot dog.

Why is a hot dog the best dog?

*Because it doesn't bite the hand that
feeds it but feeds the one that bites it.*

Why is the Dracula family so close?

Because blood is thicker than water.

What fruit has been known since
the beginning of time?

Dates.

What cake is as
hard as a rock?

*Marble
cake.*

Riddles for Thinkers

What can be caught and
heard but never seen?

A remark.

What can be measured but has no
length, width, or thickness?

The temperature.

What gets harder to catch
the faster you run?

Your breath.

What's the difference between
a dog and a gossip?

*One has a wagging tail, the
other a wagging tongue.*

Why does a dog wag his tail?

*Because no one else
will wag it for him.*

How long should a person's legs be?

Long enough to reach the ground.

What gets wetter the more it dries?

A towel.

What has six legs, but
walks with only four?

A horse with a rider.

When is longhand quicker than shorthand?

On a clock.

Would you rather an elephant
attacked you or a gorilla?

I'd rather he attacked the gorilla.

How does an elephant
get down from a tree?

*He sits on a leaf and
waits for the fall.*

When is your mind like a rumpled bed?

When it isn't made up yet.

On the way to a water hole a zebra met six giraffes. Each giraffe had three monkeys hanging from its neck. Each monkey had two birds on its tail. How many animals were going to the water hole?

Only the zebra. All the rest were coming back.

Who invented the first airplane that didn't fly?

The Wrong Brothers.

What did the sardine call
the submarine?

> *A can with people in it.*

How many legs does a mule have
if you call its tail a leg?

> *Four. Calling a tail a leg*
> *doesn't make it one.*

What can you break
with only one word?

> *Silence.*

What has cities with no houses, rivers
without water, and forests without trees?

> *A map.*

What flies when it's on and floats when it's off?

> *A feather.*

What has a mouth but can't talk?

A jar.

Almost everyone needs it, asks for it, gives it, but almost nobody takes it. What is it?

Advice.

What's brought to the table and cut, but never eaten?

A deck of cards.

Why is a poor friend better than a rich one?

Because a friend in need is a friend indeed.

Why is it interesting to study mummies?

Because you can get so wrapped up in them.

With what vegetable do you throw away the outside, cook the inside, eat the outside, and throw away the inside?

Corn on the cob.

What kind of tea helps you feel brave?

Safety.

Why do mother kangaroos hate rainy days?

Because then the children have to play inside.

How do we know the deer and the antelope are optimistic?

Because they seldom heard a discouraging word.

How can you tell the difference between trees?

Listen to their barks.

What can't you see that is always before you?

The future.

What can you hold without your hands?

Your breath.

What can you give away and still keep?

A cold.

When is it correct to say, "I is?"

"I is the letter after H."

What word allows you to take away two letters and get one?

Alone.

What's boiled then cooled,
sweetened then soured?

Iced tea with lemon.

If five cats catch five mice in five
minutes, how long will it take
one cat to catch a mouse?

Five minutes.

The more you crack it, the more
people like you. What is it?

A smile.

What comes from a tree
and fights cavities?

A toothpick.

What's the
beginning of
eternity,
The end of time
and space;
The beginning of
every end,
And the end of
every race?

The letter E.

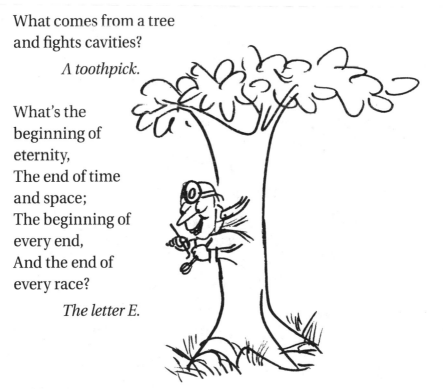

Why do dogs scratch themselves?

Because they're the only ones who know where it itches.

Why didn't the skeleton kid want to go to school?

Because his heart wasn't in it.

What dress does everyone have but no one wears?

Address.

What has no beginning or end and nothing in the middle?

A doughnut.

What's neither inside a house nor outside a house, but no house would be complete without it?

A window.

The more there is of it, the
less you see it. What is it?

Darkness.

Name five days of the week without saying:
Monday, Tuesday, Wednesday, Thursday, Friday.

*The day before yesterday, yesterday, today,
tomorrow, the day after tomorrow.*

What overpowers you—
without hurting you?

Sleep.

What's the first thing ghosts do
when they get in a car?

They boo-ckle up.

A doctor and a boy were fishing. The boy
was the doctor's son, but the doctor wasn't
the boy's father. Who was the doctor?

His mother.

A man had twelve sheep. All
but nine died. How many
sheep did he have left?

Nine.

How do you get down from an elephant?

*You don't get down from an elephant;
you get down from a duck.*

If you count twenty houses on your right going to school, and twenty houses on your left coming home, how many houses in all have you counted?

Twenty. You counted the same houses going and coming.

How many months have twenty-eight days?

All of them.

What walks on four legs in the morning, two at noon, and three in the evening?

Man. He goes on all fours as a baby, on two feet when he is grown, and uses a cane in old age. (This is the oldest known riddle in the world. It was posed by the Sphinx in ancient Greek mythology and answered by Oedipus.)

Where does satisfaction come from?

From a satisfactory.

If you had a million dollars and gave away one quarter, and another quarter, and then another quarter, how much would you have left?

A million dollars minus seventy-five cents.

Some ducks were walking down a path. There was a duck in front of two ducks, a duck behind two ducks, and a duck between two ducks. How many ducks were there in all?

Three ducks, waddling single file.

What's very light but can't be lifted?

A bubble.

What doesn't exist but has a name?

Nothing.

How can you leave a room with two legs and return with six legs?

Bring a chair back with you.

A man started to town with a fox, a goose, and a sack of corn. He came to a stream which he had to cross in a tiny boat. He could only take one across at a time. He could not leave the fox alone with the goose or the goose alone with the corn. How did he get them all safely over the stream?

He took the goose over first and came back. Then he took the fox across and brought the goose back. Next he took the corn over. He came back alone and took the goose.

What word can you pronounce quicker by adding a syllable to it?

Quick.

What's black when you buy it, red as you use it, and grey when you throw it out?

Coal.

What has two arms, two wings, two tails, three heads, three bodies and eight legs?

A man on a horse holding a chicken.

What's filled every morning and emptied every night, except once a year when it's filled at night and emptied in the morning?

A stocking.

When the dog lover put his hand in
the dog's mouth to see how many
teeth it had, what did the dog do?

*The dog closed its mouth to see how
many fingers the dog lover had.*

What cannot be seen but
only heard, and will not
speak unless it is spoken to?

An echo.

Who is it that everybody listens
to but nobody believes?

The weatherman.

What's easy to get into but
hard to get out of?

Trouble.

What's pronounced like one letter, written with
three letters, and belongs to all animals?

Eye.

Why do you always find something
in the last place you look?

Because when you find it, you stop looking.

Why do we say "amen" and not "awomen?"

*Because we sing
"hymns," not "hers."*

What grows larger the
more you take away?

A hole.

What rises in the morning and waves all day?

A flag.

Which two letters of the
alphabet are nothing?

MT.

What's the difference between the
rising and the setting sun?

A day.

What's always coming
but never arrives?

Tomorrow.

What relation is a loaf of bread to a locomotive?

*Mother. Bread is a necessity, a
locomotive is an invention, and
"Necessity is the mother of invention."*

What is it that you can take away the
whole from and still have some left?

The word "wholesome."

What's heavier in warm weather than in winter?

Traffic to the beach.

How did rich people
get their money?

*They were calm
and collected.*

5

That's Ridiculous

How do you make an elephant laugh?

Tickle its ivories.

How do you make an elephant stew?

Keep it waiting for two hours.

How can you tell an elephant from spaghetti?

*The elephant doesn't slip off
the end of your fork.*

What kind of geese are
found in Portugal?

Portu-geese.

What do geese get when
they eat too much cake?

Goose pimples.

What do you get if you cross a
rhinoceros and a goose?

*An animal that honks before
it runs you over.*

How do you run over an elephant?

*Climb up its tail, dash to its
head, and slide down its trunk.*

What's green and jumps three
feet every five seconds?

A frog with hiccups.

What did the Martian say to the gas pump?

*"Take your finger out of your
ear and listen to me!"*

What do you get if
you cross a crocodile
with an abalone?

*You get a
crocabalone.*

What do you get if you blow your
hair dryer down a rabbit hole?

Hot cross bunnies.

What's green, and has two legs and a trunk?

A seasick tourist.

What's a monster's normal eyesight?

20-20-20-20-20.

How does
a monster
count to 18?

*On its
fingers.*

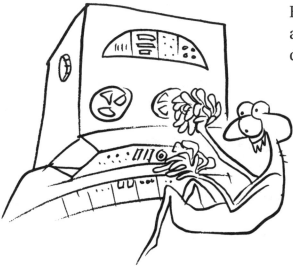

What do ghosts chew?

Boo-ble gum.

When do comedians take
milk and sugar?

At tea-hee time.

What cuts lawns and gives milk?

A lawn moo-er.

What shampoo do mountains use?

Head and Boulders.

What comes in different flavors
and colors and makes music?

Cello pudding.

Where does the Gingerbread
Man sleep?

Under a cookie sheet.

What weighs two tons,
feels cold to the touch,
and comes on a stick?

A hippo-popsicle.

What happens when you phone a bee?

You get a buzzy signal.

Where do they serve snacks to football players?

In the Soup-er Bowl.

What's the fastest way to make
soup taste terrible?

> *Change the U to an A, and you get soap.*

What do you get when you use
soap and water on the stove?

> *Foam on the range.*

What would you get if you crossed a
noisy frog and a shaggy dog?

> *A croaker spaniel.*

What reaction do you get when
you tell stomach jokes?

> *Belly laughs.*

Why did the banana split?

> *Because it saw the bread box, the
> milk shake, and the ginger snap.*

What time is it when it's halfway
between the "tick" and the "tock"?

> *Half past ticks o'tock.*

What did the duck say when it finished shopping?

"Just put it on my bill."

What game do baby chickens play?

Peck-a-boo.

How do you tell the difference between a rooster and a hen?

Throw a bird some seeds. If he eats it, it's a rooster; if she eats it, it's a hen.

How do you straighten crooked apple trees?

You send them to an orchardontist.

What do you get if you cross a small horn and a little flute?

A tootie flooty.

What's the best way to clean an aardvark?

With an aardvarkuum cleaner.

What color is a happy cat?

Purrple.

What do you get if you cross a
parrot with a bumble bee?

*A flying creature that talks about
how busy it is all the time.*

What would happen if you crossed
a turkey with a centipede?

*At Thanksgiving, everybody
would get a drumstick.*

Where is a sneeze usually pointed?

Atchoo!

Who performs the operations
in a fish hospital?

The head sturgeon.

What operation was named for Charles de Gaulle?

De-gall stone operation.

When is it good manners to spit in a man's face?

When his mustache is on fire.

Trick or Treat!

What do canaries say
on Halloween?

"Twick or tweet!"

What loses its head every morning
but gets it back at night?

A pillow.

Are rabbits underpaid?

Yes. They work for a small celery

What do squirrels give each
other on Valentine's Day?

Forget-me-nuts.

What should you do with a
prune that's a year old?

Give it a birthday party.

What caused the riot in the post office?

A stampede.

What pillar is never used to hold up a building?

A caterpillar.

What did the boy snake
say to the girl snake?

"Give me a little hiss."

What would you get if you crossed
a gorilla and a skunk?

I don't know what you'd call it,
but it wouldn't have any trouble
getting a seat on the bus.

What insect can't
say yes or no?

A may-bee.

What comes out at night and goes "Flap! Flap! Chomp! Ouch!"

A vampire with a sore tooth.

What kind of dreams does a plumber have?

Pipe dreams.

What person makes a living by talking to himself?

A ventriloquist.

What kinds of toys does a psychiatrist's child play with?

Mental blocks.

What do you get if you cross poison ivy with a four-leaf clover?

You get a rash of good luck.

What's the difference between a ball and a prince?

One is thrown to the air; the other is heir to the throne.

How do you kiss a hockey player?

You pucker up.

Who do mermaids date?

They go out with the tide.

Why is it hard to recognize horses from the back?

*Because they're always
switching their tails.*

What's a shark's favorite
flavor of ice cream?

Sharkolate.

What character got all his work done by Friday?

Robinson Crusoe.

What do frogs drink at parties?

Croak-a-Cola.

How did the ditch digger get his job?

He just fell into it.

Which is less intelligent   a large
chicken or a small chicken?

The large one is the bigger cluck.

What do you get if you cross an
elephant and a computer?

*A ten thousand pound
know-it-all.*

What's the noisiest thing in space?

Shooting stars.

What do you find more in sorrow than in anger?

The letter R.

What makes a chess player happy?

Taking a knight off.

Where do ghosts get their mail?

At the dead-letter office.

What's a ghost's
favorite food?

Spookghetti.

What do you call the
sweetheart of a ghoul?

A ghoul friend.

What do you call a vampire who
stays up while the sun is out?

An all-day sucker.

How can you tell if a vampire has
been in your tomato juice?

By the tooth marks on the can.

What does an up-to-date witch fly?

An electric broom.

What happened to the woman who
covered herself with vanishing cream?

Nobody knows.

What do you get if you
cross an owl and a skunk?

*An animal that
smells bad, but
doesn't give a hoot.*

What geometric figure do sailors fear?

The Bermuda Triangle.

Why is a leaking faucet
like a horse race?

It's off and running.

What do you get if you cross
a potato and a sponge?

*A vegetable that soaks
up lots of gravy.*

What do you get if you cross
chewing gum with a yo-yo?

*I don't know, but if you swallow it
by mistake, it comes up again.*

What kind of
bars can't keep
prisoners in jail?

*Chocolate
bars.*

Did you hear the joke about
the chocolate cake?

Never mind, it's too rich.

What would you get if you stacked thousands of pizza pies on top of each other?

A leaning tower of pizza.

What's a pizza's favorite means of transportation?

Pie-cycle.

Where do cows go for entertainment?

To the mooovies.

7

Hyde & Sick

How do creatures from outer space drink their tea?

From flying saucers.

Why doesn't a frog jump when it's sad?

It's too unhoppy.

How can you tell a person's age?

Read between the lines.

What happens if you swallow a doorknob?

Your stomach keeps turning.

What would happen if you cut your left side off?

You'd be all right.

What's the difference between a
pitchfork and a toothpick?

*Well, if you don't know, you'd
better not pick your teeth.*

Why shouldn't you brush your
teeth with gunpowder?

You might shoot your mouth off.

When the baby cries at night, who gets up?

The whole neighborhood.

Where does a watchmaker
take his sick watches?

To the tick doc.

What happens when you stare
at a watch too long?

You get clock-eyed.

What did the bored cow say as
she got up in the morning?

"Just an udder day."

Why did the cow go
to the psychiatrist?

*Because it had a
fodder complex.*

Why didn't the dentist laugh at the joke about the sore tooth?

Because he hurt that one before.

What's the difference between an elephant and an absent-minded professor?

The elephant doesn't forget.

Name a healthy laugh.

A hardy ha-ha.

What do you get if a dinosaur steps on your foot?

Anklosaurus.

What do you get if you cross a
popular musician and a shark?

Rockjaw.

How long should a doctor practice medicine?

Until he gets it right.

What's gray and blue and very big?

An elephant holding its breath.

What do you call a skeleton
that won't get out of bed?

Lazy bones.

Where do goblins go when they get sick?

To the witch doctor.

Why is doing nothing
so tiring?

*Because you can't
stop and rest.*

What disease does a vampire fear most?

Tooth decay.

What did the surgeon say to the patient
who complained about his operation?

"Next time, suture self!"

How can you touch the floor without standing on your feet or hands?

Fall out of bed.

What made the farmer yell?

Someone stepped on his corn.

What happens when corn catches cold?

It gets an ear ache.

What disease does grass get?

Hay fever.

What's stormy weather for mice and rats?

When it rains cats and dogs.

When does a lion relax?

When it's lion down.

How do tailors feel when they're neither happy nor unhappy?

Sew-sew.

How can you avoid being driven crazy?

Walk.

What's the difference between ammonia and pneumonia?

Ammonia comes in bottles, pneumonia comes in chests.

What happens to you when you're hit by a Wells Fargo express wagon?

You're stage struck.

What do you give to a sick bird?

First-aid tweetment.

Where do you send a sick pony?

To the horse-pital.

What did one elevator say to the other elevator?

"I think I'm coming down with something."

Why did the house call for a doctor?

Because it had windowpanes.

What should you do if you find yourself
with water on the knee, water on the
elbow, and water on the brain?

Turn off the shower.

Why was the fireplace in the hospital?

Because it had a hearth attack.

What injury do Olympic athletes suffer?

A slipped discus.

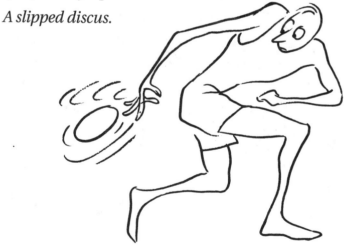

What do Eskimos get under their
eyes when they can't sleep?

Arctic circles.

8

Plain Crazy

What do you call a person who
thinks he has wings and can fly?

Plane crazy.

What kind of fish do they serve on airplanes?

Flying fish.

Where do pilots keep their personal things?

In air pockets.

When is a man like a suit of clothes?

*When his tongue has a coat and
his breath comes in short pants.*

What does an octopus wear?

A coat of arms.

Why are fish poor tennis players?

*Because they don't like
to get close to the net.*

What kind of illumination did
Noah use on the ark?

Floodlights.

Do Cadillacs stretch?

No, but Mercedes Benz.

What's black and white and has sixteen wheels?

A zebra on roller skates.

What's black and wrinkled and makes pit stops?

A racing prune.

How do Martian cowboys signal each other?

With communication saddle lights.

What do you get if you cross
a galaxy and a toad?

Star warts.

If you saw nine elephants walking
down the street with red socks and one
elephant walking down the street with
green socks, what would this prove?

*That nine out of ten elephants
wear red socks.*

How can you tell if an
elephant is visiting
your house?

*His tricycle will be
parked outside.*

Name ten African animals in three seconds?

Nine lions and a giraffe.

What does Tarzan sing
at Christmas time?

"Jungle Bells."

When is it dangerous to play cards in the jungle?

When the joker's wild.

Why did the dentist throw away
his electric toothbrush?

*Because none of his patients
had electric teeth.*

What kind of teeth can you buy for a dollar?

Buck teeth.

What use is a reindeer?

To make the flowers grow, sweetie.

How do you serve toffee?

In toffee tups.

How can you tell which
end of a worm is its head?

*Tickle it in the
middle and see
which end laughs.*

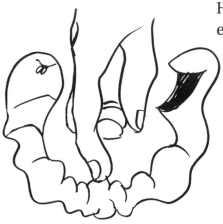

What does a tuba
call his father?

*Oom-
papa.*

A man opened a piece of furniture and a
dozen people fell out. How could that be?

It was a missing persons bureau.

Where do cows go for their vacation?

To Cowlifornia.

What do cows use for money?

Moola.

What does a silly cow
say when it's milked?

"Udder nonsense."

What would you get if you crossed
a rabbit and a lawn sprinkler?

Hare spray.

What would you get if you crossed a
vampire bat and a magician?

A flying sorcerer.

What would you get if
you crossed a newborn
snake with a basketball?

*You'd get a bouncing
baby boa.*

Why did the chicken cross the road?

Because the light was green.

Why did the chicken
sit on the axe?

*So she could
hatch-et.*

What would you get if you crossed peanut
butter, bread, jelly, and a werewolf?

*You would get a hairy peanut butter
sandwich that howls when the moon is full.*

What close relatives do boy robots have?

Transistors.

How do you make a hamburger roll?

*Take it to the top of a steep
hill and give it a shove.*

What kind of cake holds water?

Sponge cake.

What kind of cake can make
you froth at the mouth?

A cake of soap.

What did the mother broom
say to her broom infant?

"Go to sweep, little baby."

What do you call a baby rifle?

A son-of-a-gun.

What did lumberjack shout when
the tree fell too soon?

"Tim . . ."

What pigs write letters to each other?

Pen pals.

What was Samuel Clemens's pen name?

He never had a name for his pen.

Why is the pen mightier than the sword?

Because no one has yet invented a ballpoint sword.

Who invented the grandfather clock?

Pendulum Franklin.

How much does a psychiatrist charge an elephant?

$50 for the visit and $500 for the couch.

Why do elephants lie down?

Because they can't lie up.

How do you keep an elephant from going through the eye of a needle?

Tie a knot in its tail.

How do you catch an electric eel?

With a lightning rod.

Why did the ding dong wring his hands?

Because his bell was out of order.

What are Van Winkle trousers?

Pants with a rip.

What's the difference between a New Yorker and a dentist?

One roots for the Yanks, the other yanks for the roots.

What kind of pickle does a dentist use?

A drill pickle.

How do you make a pickle laugh?

Tell it an elephant joke.

Mad Manners

What's the best thing to do if
you find a gorilla in your bed?

Sleep somewhere else.

What do you call a gorilla
with cotton in his ears?

Anything you want.
He can't hear you.

What do you say to King Kong
when he gets married?

Kong-ratulations!

What do you call a carpenter
who misplaces his tools?

A saw loser.

Why should you never mention the number 288 in front of the principal?

Because it's two gross.

How mad can a kangaroo get?

Hopping mad!

What does a match do when it loses its temper?

It flares up.

If a chicken crosses the road, rolls in the mud, and crosses back again, what is it?

A dirty double-crosser.

What do you get if you cross a homing pigeon and a parrot?

A bird that asks the way home if it gets lost.

What bird is most hygienic?

The rooster. He won't lend anybody his comb.

Is it all right to scream when the tailor presses your pants?

Yes, if you're still in them.

What's the difference between shillings and pence?

You can walk down the street without shillings.

What's the quickest way to get ahead as an electrician?

Pull wires.

What do you get if you cross a shark with a parrot?

An animal that talks your ear off.

What do you get if you cross a canary and an elephant?

A pretty messy cage.

What kind of word could you take to tea parties?

A proper noun.

What does an electric rabbit say?

"Watts up, Doc?"

How do most people learn to play the violin?

From scratch.

What does the voice
of experience say?

"Ouch!"

What's the best way to improve a long speech?

Use shortening.

What did one raindrop say to the other?

"Two's company and three's a cloud."

Why does time fly?

*To get away from all the people
who are trying to kill it.*

What plants are the most greedy?

*Weeds. Give them an inch
and they'll take a yard.*

When is the best time to milk a cow?

When she is in the moo-d.

Why did the surgeon wear a tuxedo
in the operating room?

*Because he always dressed
formally for an opening.*

On what day are ghosts allowed to make noise?

Moan-day.

Why do demons and
ghouls get along so well?

*Because demons are
a ghoul's best friend.*

What happens when you ask an
oyster a personal question?

It clams up.

Why are giraffes so slow to apologize?

*It takes a long time for them
to swallow their pride.*

How does taking a ferry boat
change people for the worse?

It makes them cross.

Why is the letter D so aggravating?

Because it makes ma mad.

Why was the
farmer angry?

*Because
someone
got his
goat.*

What's the correct way to file an ax?
Under the letter A.

What kind of tea do the king and queen drink?
Royalty.

What does a hungry
mathematician like to eat?
A square meal.

Where does success come before work?
In the dictionary.

What should you do if
you meet King Kong?
*Give him a big
banana.*

Why are bananas popular?

Because they have a-peel.

What do you call a 2,000 pound gorilla?

"Sir."

What kind of tool do you use
to fix a broken gorilla?

A monkey wrench.

What song does a violinist sing to his violin?

"I've got you under my chin . . ."

What's the favorite song of the bees?

*"Bee it ever so bumble,
there's no place like comb . . ."*

Why did the teacher excuse the little firefly?

*Because when you've got to
glow, you've got to glow.*

KNOCK-KNOCKS

A

Knock-knock.
Who's there?
Abyssinia.
Abyssinia who?
Abyssinia behind bars one of these days.

Knock-knock.
Who's there?
Acid.
Acid who?
Acid down and be quiet!

Knock-knock.
Who's there?
Adelia.
Adelia who?
Adelia the cards after
you cut the deck.

Knock-knock.
Who's there?
Adlai.
Adlai
Adlai a bet on that.

Knock-knock.
Who's there?
Agatha.
Agatha who?
Agatha headache. Do you have an aspirin?

Knock-knock.
Who's there?
Aida.
Aida who?
Aida lot of candy and now
my stomach aches.

Knock-knock.
Who's there?
Alpaca.
Alpaca who?
Alpaca the trunk, you pack-a the suitcase.

Knock-knock.
Who's there?
Amahl.
Amahl who?
Amahl shook up.

Knock-knock.
Who's there?
Amana.
Amana who?
Amana bad mood!

Knock-knock.
Who's there?
Ammonia.
Ammonia who?
Ammonia little kid.

Knock-knock.
Who's there?
Amos.
Amos who?
Amos-quito bit me.

Knock-knock.
Who's there?
Andy.
Andy who?
Andy bit me again.

Knock-knock.
Who's there?
Arizona.
Arizona who?
Arizona room for one of us in this neighborhood.

Knock-knock.
Who's there?
Armenia.
Armenia who?
Armenia every word I say.

Knock-knock.
Who's there?
Arnold.
Arnold who?
Arnold friend from Transylvania.

Knock-knock.
Who's there?
Samoa.
Samoa who?
Samoa old friends from
Transylvania.

Knock-knock.
Who's there?
Arthur.
Arthur who?
Arthur anymore at home like you?

Knock-knock.
Who's there?
Ashley.
Ashley who?
Ashleyt's foot.

Knock-knock.
Who's there?
Asia.
Asia who?
Asia going to invite me in?

Knock-knock.
Who's there?
Athena.
Athena who?
Athena flying saucer!

Knock-knock.
Who's there?
Atlas.
Atlas who?
Atlas it's Friday.

Knock-knock.
Who's there?
Atomic.
Atomic who?
Atomic ache.

Knock-knock.
Who's there?
Aunt Lou.
Aunt Lou who?
Aunt Lou do you think you are?

Knock-knock.
Who's there?
Avenue.
Avenue who?
Avenue heard the good news?

Knock-knock.
Who's there?
Banana.
Banana who?

Knock-knock.
Who's there?
Banana.
Banana who?

Knock-knock.
Who's there?
Banana.
Banana who?

Knock-knock.
Who's there?
Orange.
Orange who?
Orange you glad I didn't
say banana?

Knock-knock.
  Who's there?
Bridget.
  Bridget who?
London Bridget.

        Knock-knock.
            Who's there?
        Brigham.
            Brigham who?
        "Brigham back my sunshine to me . . ."

Knock-knock.
  Who's there?
Burton.
  Burton who?
Burton the hand is worth two in the bush.

Knock-knock.
Who's there?
Butch.
Butch who?
Butch your arms around me.

Knock-knock.
Who's there?
Butcher.
Butcher who?
Butcher money where your mouth is.

Knock-knock.
Who's there?
Button.
Button who?
Button in is not polite.

C

Knock-knock.
Who's there?
Candy.
Candy who?
Candy cow jump over the moon?

Knock-knock.
Who's there?
Cantaloupe.
Cantaloupe who?
Cantaloupe today.

Knock-knock.
Who's there?
Lettuce.
Lettuce who?
Lettuce try tomorrow.

Knock-knock.
Who's there?
Carmen.
Carmen who?
Carmen get it!

Knock-knock.
Who's there?
Cash.
Cash who?
I knew you were some kind of nut.

Knock-knock.
Who's there?
Cecil.
Cecil who?
"Cecil have music wherever she goes . . ."

Knock-knock.
Who's there?
Celeste.
Celeste who?
Celeste time I'm going
to tell you this.

Knock-knock.
Who's there?
Cello.
Cello who?
Cello dere!

Knock-knock.
Who's there?
Cereal.
Cereal who?
Cereal pleasure to meet you.

Knock-knock.
Who's there?
Cozy.
Cozy who?
Cozy who's knocking.

Knock-knock.
Who's there?
Custer.
Custer who?
Custer a penny to find out.

Knock-knock.
Who's there?
Cynthia.
Cynthia who?
Cynthia been away, I've been so sad.

D

Knock-knock.
   Who's there?
Daisy.
   Daisy who?
Daisy plays, nights he sleeps.

Knock-knock.
   Who's there?
Dana.
   Dana who?
Dana talk with your mouth full.

Knock-knock.
   Who's there?
Darius.
Darius who?
Darius a lot I have to tell you.

Knock-knock.
  Who's there?
Darren.
  Darren who?
Darren young man on
the flying trapeze.

Knock-knock.
  Who's there?
Dennis.
  Dennis who?
Dennis says I've got a cavity.

Knock-knock.
Who's there?
Denver.
Denver who?
Denver the good old days.

Knock-knock.
Who's there?
Desiree.
Desiree who?
Desiree of sunshine in my life.

Knock-knock.
Who's there?
Dewey.
Dewey who?
Dewey have to keep telling knock-knock jokes?

Knock-knock.
Who's there?
DeWitt.
DeWitt who?
DeWitt now or never.

Knock-knock.
Who's there?
Diesel.
Diesel who?
Diesel teach me
to go around knocking
on doors.

Knock-knock.
Who's there?
Dimension.
Dimension who?
Dimension it.

Knock-knock.
Who's there?
Dinah.
Dinah who?
"Dinah shoot until you see the whites of their eyes."

Knock-knock.
Who's there?
Dino.
Dino who?
Dino the answer.

Knock-knock.
Who's there?
Alaska.
Alaska who?
Alaska my mother.

Knock-knock.
Who's there?
Diploma.
Diploma who?
Diploma can fix the leak.

Knock-knock.
Who's there?
Disaster.
Disaster who?
Disaster be my lucky day!

Knock-knock.
    Who's there?
Disguise.
    Disguise who?
Disguise the limit.

Knock-knock.
    Who's there?
Dishes.
    Dishes who?
Dishes the end of the road.

Knock-knock.
    Who's there?
Disk.
    Disk who?
Disk is a recorded message.

Knock-knock.
    Who's there?
Dustin
    Dustin who?
Dustin off my welcome mat for you.

Knock-knock.
    Who's there?
Dwayne.
    Dwayne who?
"Dwayne in Spain falls
mainly on the plain . . ."

Knock-knock.
Who's there?
Dwight.
Dwight who?
Dwight way and the wrong way.

E

Knock-knock.
  Who's there?
Earl.
  Earl who?
Earl be glad to tell you if you open the door.

  Knock-knock.
    Who's there?
  Ears.
    Ears who?
  Ears looking at you!

Knock-knock.
  Who's there?
Eddie.
  Eddie who?
Eddie body home?

Knock-knock.
Who's there?
Elke.
Elke who?
"Elke Seltzer ...Plop, plop, fizz, fizz ..."

Knock-knock.
Who's there?
Ella.
Ella who?
Ella-vator. Doesn't that give you a lift?

Knock-knock.
Who's there?
Ella Mann.
Ella Mann who?
Ella Mann-tary, my dear Watson.

Knock-knock.
Who's there?
Ellen.
Ellen who?
Ellen-eed is love.

Knock-knock.
Who's there?
Elsie.
Elsie who?
Elsie you around.

Knock-knock.
Who's there?
Emma.
Emma who?
Emma glad you asked that.

Knock-knock.
Who's there?
Emmett.
Emmett who?
Emmett your service.

Knock-knock.
Who's there?
Enoch.
Enoch who?
Enoch and Enoch but nobody
opens the door.

Knock-knock.
Who's there?
Esther.
Esther who?
Esther anything I
can do for you?

Knock-knock.
   Who's there?
Eva.
   Eva who?
Eva I told you, would you let me in?

                    Knock-knock.
                       Who's there?
                    Ezra.
                       Ezra who?
                    Ezra no hope for me?

Knock-knock.
Who's there?
Fanny.
Fanny who?
Fanny-body home?

Knock-knock.
Who's there?
Farley.
Farley who?
Farley the leader.

Knock-knock.
Who's there?
Ferdie.
Ferdie who?
Ferdie last time, open the door!

Knock-knock.
Who's there?
Fiddlesticks.
Fiddlesticks who?
Fiddlesticks out if the
blanket's too short.

Knock-knock.
Who's there?
Fletcher.
Fletcher who?
Fletcher self go!

Knock-knock.
Who's there?
Franz.
Franz who?
"Franz, Romans, countrymen ..."

Knock-knock.
Who's there?
Freddie.
Freddie who?
Freddie or not, here I come.

Knock-knock.
Who's there?
Freighter.
Freighter who?
Freighter open the door?

Knock-knock.
Who's there?
Fresno.
Fresno who?
"Rudolf the Fresno reindeer . . ."

G

Knock-knock.
Who's there?
Genoa.
Genoa who?
Genoa new knock-knock joke?

Knock-knock.
Who's there?
Gerald.
Gerald who?
Gerald washed up, kid.

Knock-knock.
Who's there?
Gladys.
Gladys who?
Gladys see you.

Knock-knock.
Who's there?
Gopher.
Gopher who?
Gopher broke.

Knock-knock.
Who's there?
Gorilla.
Gorilla who?
Gorilla cheese sandwich.

Knock-knock.
Who's there?
Grammar.
Grammar who?
Grammar crackers.

Knock-knock.
Who's there?
Greta.
Greta who?
You Greta my nerves.

Knock-knock.
Who's there?
Guinevere.
Guinevere who?
Guinevere going to get together?

Knock-knock.
   Who's there?
Guthrie.
   Guthrie who?
Guthrie blind mice.

H

Knock-knock.
Who's there?
Hacienda.
Hacienda who?
Hacienda the story.

Knock-knock.
Who's there?
Hagar.
Hagar who?
"Hagar, you with the stars
in your eyes . . ."

Knock-knock.
Who's there?
Hair.
Hair who?
Hair today, gone tomorrow.

Knock-knock.
Who's there?
Handsome.
Handsome who?
Handsome pretzel sticks through the
keyhole, and I'll tell you more.

Knock-knock.
Who's there?
Heaven.
Heaven who?
Heaven seen you for a long time.

Knock-knock.
Who's there?
Heidi.
Heidi who?
Heidi-clare you look great!

Knock-knock.
Who's there?
Heifer.
Heifer who?
Heifer cow is better than none.

Knock-knock.
  Who's there?
Hiram.
  Hiram who?
Hiram fine, how are you?

Knock-knock.
  Who's there?
Hoffman.
  Hoffman who?
"I'll Hoffman, I'll puff, and I'll blow your house down."

Knock-knock.
  Who's there?
Hollis.
  Hollis who?
Hollis forgiven. Come home.

Knock-knock.
    Who's there?
Homer.
    Homer who?
Homer-gain.

Knock-knock.
    Who's there?
Hominy.
    Hominy who?
Hominy times are we going through this?

I

Knock-knock.
   Who's there?
Ice cream soda.
   Ice cream soda who?
Ice cream soda whole world
will know what I think.

   Knock-knock.
      Who's there?
   Ichabod.
      Ichabod who?
   Ichabod night out.
   Can I borrow your
   umbrella?

Knock-knock.
   Who's there?
Igloo.
   Igloo who?
"Igloo knew Suzie like I know Suzie …"

. . ,,

Knock-knock.
Who's there?
Iguana.
Iguana who?
"Iguana hold
your hand …"

Knock-knock.
Who's there?
Ike.
Ike who?
Ike-n't stop laughing.

Knock-knock.
Who's there?
Ilona.
Ilona who?
Ilona Ranger.

Knock-knock.
Who's there?
Ivory.
Ivory who?
Ivory strong like Tarzan.

Knock-knock.
Who's there?
Izzy.
Izzy who?
Izzy come, Izzy go.

Knock-knock.
Who's there?
Jaguar.
Jaguar who?
"Jaguar nimble, Jaguar quick."

Knock-knock.
Who's there?
Jamaica.
Jamaica who?
Jamaica mistake?

Knock-knock.
Who's there?
Jaws.
Jaws who?
Jaws truly.

Knock-knock.
Who's there?
Jerrold.
Jerrold who?
Jerrold friend, that's who!

Knock-knock.
Who's there?
Jess.
Jess who?
Jess one of those things.

Knock-knock.
Who's there?
Jester.
Jester who?
Jester minute, pardner.

Knock-knock.
Who's there?
Jethro.
Jethro who?
Jethro the boat and
stop talking so much.

Knock-knock.
Who's there?
Jewel.
Jewel who?
Jewel remember me after you see my face.

Knock-knock.
Who's there?
Joan.
Joan who?
Joan call us, we'll call you.

Knock-knock.
Who's there?
Joanne.
Joanne who?
Joanne tell.

Knock-knock.
Who's there?
Joe Namath.
Joe Namath who?
Joe Namath not on the door.
That's why I knocked.

Knock-knock.
Who's there?
Amy Namath.
Amy Namath who?
"Amy Namath Alice and my husband's name is Al . . ."

Knock-knock.
> *Who's there?*

Justice.
> *Justice who?*

Justice I thought.
No one's home.

Knock-knock.
> *Who's there?*

Justin.
> *Justin who?*

Justin case.

K

Knock-knock.
>   *Who's there?*
Kaye.
>   *Kaye who?*
"Kaye será será."

Knock-knock.
>   *Who's there?*
Kent.
>   *Kent who?*
Kent you tell who it is?

Knock-knock.
>   *Who's there?*
Kipper.
>   *Kipper who?*
Kipper hands
to yourself.

L

Knock-knock.
Who's there?
Lauren.
Lauren who?
Lauren order.

Knock-knock.
Who's there?
Leif.
Leif who?
Leif me alone.

Knock-knock.
Who's there?
Lena.
Lena who?
Lena little closer. I have a secret to tell you.

Knock-knock.
Who's there?
Lucretia.
Lucretia who?
Lucretia from the Black Lagoon.

Knock-knock.
Who's there?
Luigi.
Luigi who?
Luigi board.

Knock-knock.
Who's there?
Luke.
Luke who?
Luke before you leap.

Knock-knock.
Who's there?
Lyndon.
Lyndon who?
Lyndon ear and I'll tell you.

M

Knock-knock.
> *Who's there?*

Major.
> *Major who?*

Major answer this knock-knock joke.

Knock-knock.
> *Who's there?*

Manuel.
> *Manuel who?*

Manuel be sorry if you
don't open this door.

Knock-knock.
> *Who's there?*

Mara.
> *Mara who?*

"Mara, Mara, on the wall . . ."

Knock-knock.
Who's there?
Midas.
Midas who?
Midas well relax. I'm not going any place.

Knock-knock.
Who's there?
Minerva.
Minerva who?
Minerva's wreck from all these questions.

Knock-knock.
Who's there?
Miniature.
Miniature who?
Miniature open your mouth, you put your foot in it.

Knock-knock.
Who's there?
Minneapolis.
Minneapolis who?
Minneapolis each day keep many doctors away.

Knock-knock.
Who's there?
Minnie.
Minnie who?
No, not Minnie-who—Minnehaha.

Knock-knock.
Who's there?
Mischa.
Mischa who?
Mischa a lot.

Knock-knock.
Who's there?
Missouri.
Missouri who?
Missouri loves company.

Knock-knock.
Who's there?
Mitzi.
Mitzi who?
Mitzi door shut, you'll never find out.

Knock-knock.
Who's there?
Monkey.
Monkey who?
Monkey won't fit, that's why I knocked.

Knock-knock.
Who's there?
Moose.
Moose who?
Moose you be so nosy?

Knock-knock.
Who's there?
Morris.
Morris who?
Morris another day.

Knock-knock.
Who's there?
Mortimer.
Mortimer who?
Mortimer than
meets the eye.

Knock-knock.
Who's there?
Muffin.
Muffin who?
Muffin grouchy in the morning

Knock-knock.
Who's there?
Myth.
Myth who?
Myth you, too.

N

Knock-knock.
> *Who's there?*

Nadya.
> *Nadya who?*

Nadya head if you understand
what I'm saying.

Knock-knock.
> *Who's there?*

Nana.
> *Nana who?*

Nana your business.

Knock-knock.
> *Who's there?*

Nettie.
> *Nettie who?*

Nettie as a fruitcake.

Knock-knock.
Who's there?
Noah.
Noah who?
"Noahbody knows the trouble I've seen . . ."

Knock-knock.
Who's there?
Norma Lee.
Norma Lee who?
Norma Lee I don't go around knocking on doors,
but I have this wonderful set of encyclopedias ...

Knock-knock.
Who's there?
Nuisance.
Nuisance who?
What's nuisance yesterday?

Knock-knock.
Who's there?
Nurse.
Nurse who?
Nurse sense in
talking to you.

O

Knock-knock.
  Who's there?
Ocelot.
  Ocelot who?
Ocelot of questions, don't you?

Knock-knock.
  Who's there?
Odette.
  Odette who?
Odette's a bad sign.

Knock-knock.
  Who's there?
Odessa.
  Odessa who?
Odessa hot one!

Knock-knock.
Who's there?
Olivia.
Olivia who?
Olivia but I forgot my key.

Knock-knock.
Who's there?
Ollie.
Ollie who?
Ollie time you say that, I wish you'd cut it out.

Knock-knock.
Who's there?
Omar.
Omar who?
Omar goodness gracious! Wrong door!

Knock-knock.
Who's there?
Omega.
Omega who?
Omega best man win!

Knock-knock.
Who's there?
Ooze.
Ooze who?
Ooze in charge around here?

Knock-knock.
Who's there?
Opera.
Opera who?
Opera-tunity. And you thought
opportunity only knocked once!

Knock-knock.
Who's there?
Orange juice.
Orange juice who?
Orange juice going
to talk to me?

Knock-knock.
Who's there?
Orson.
Orson who?
Orson around again?

Knock-knock.
Who's there?
Orson.
Orson who?
Orson buggy is about your speed.

Knock-knock.
  Who's there?
Osborn.
  Osborn who?
Osborn today—it's my birthday!

$\mathcal{P}$

Knock-knock.
   Who's there?
Passion.
   Passion who?
Passion by and thought
I'd say hello.

Knock-knock.
   Who's there?
Pasture.
   Pasture who?
Pasture bedtime, isn't it?

Knock-knock.
   Who's there?
Pecan.
   Pecan who?
Pecan somebody your own size!

Knock-knock.
Who's there?
Pharaoh.
Pharaoh who?
Pharaoh 'nuff.

Knock-knock.
Who's there?
Phineas.
Phineas who?
"Phineas thing happened to me today . . ."

Knock-knock.
Who's there?
Philippa.
Philippa who?
Philippa bathtub. I'm dirty.

Knock-knock.
Who's there?
Phyllis.
Phyllis who?
Phyllis in on the news.

Knock-knock.
Who's there?
Ping pong.
Ping pong who?
"Ping pong, the witch is dead . . ."

Knock-knock.
*Who's
there?*
Plato.
*Plato
who?*
Plato spaghetti and meatballs, please.

Knock-knock.
Who's there?
Police.
Police who?
Police open the door.

Q

Knock-knock.
Who's there?
Quacker.
Quacker who?
Quacker 'nother bad
joke and I'm leaving.

Knock-knock.
Who's there?
Quebec.
Quebec who?
Quebec to the
end of the line.

Knock-knock.
Who's there?
Quiet Tina.
Quiet Tina who?
"Quiet Tina courtroom—monkey wants to speak."

R

Knock-knock.
> *Who's there?*
Rabbit.
> *Rabbit who?*
Rabbit up neatly. It's a present.

> Knock-knock.
> > *Who's there?*
> Raleigh.
> > *Raleigh who?*
> Raleigh round the flag, boys.

Knock-knock.
> *Who's there?*
Rapunzel.
> *Rapunzel who?*
"Rapunzel troubles in your old kit bag
and smile, smile, smile …"

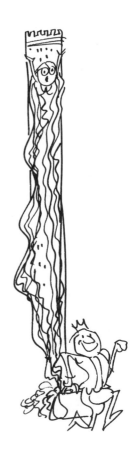

Knock-knock.
Who's there?
Razor.
Razor who?
Razor hands—this is a stick-up!

Knock-knock.
Who's there?
Red.
Red who?
Red peppers. Isn't that a hot one?

Knock-knock.
Who's there?
Rhoda.
Rhoda who?
"Row, row, Rhoda boat . . ."

Knock-knock.
Who's there?
Robin.
Robin who?
Robin the piggy bank again?

Knock-knock.
Who's there?
Rocky.
Rocky who?
"Rocky bye baby on the tree top . . ."

Knock-knock.
Who's there?
Roland.
Roland who?
"Roland stone gathers no moss."

Knock-knock.
Who's there?
Rona.
Rona who?
Rona the mill.

Knock-knock.
Who's there?
Roxanne.
Roxanne who?
Roxanne your head or something?

Knock-knock.
Who's there?
Rufus.
Rufus who?
Rufus leaking and
I'm getting wet.

Knock-knock.
  Who's there?
Sabina.
  Sabina who?
Sabina long time since I've seen you.

Knock-knock.
  Who's there?
Mischa.
  Mischa who?
Mischa a lot.

Knock-knock.
  Who's there?
Sacha.
  Sacha who?
Sacha fuss, just because I
knocked at your door.

Knock-knock.
Who's there?
Schatzi.
Schatzi who?
Schatzi way the ball bounces.

Knock-knock.
Who's there?
Scissor.
Scissor who?
Scissor and Cleopatra.

Knock-knock.
Who's there?
Scold.
Scold who?
Scold outside.

Knock-knock.
Who's there?
Seymour.
Seymour who?
Seymour if you'd get the door open.

Knock-knock.
Who's there?
Sharon.
Sharon who?
Sharon share alike.

Knock-knock.
Who's there?
Sheila.
Sheila who?
"Sheila be coming round the mountain when she comes ..."

Knock-knock.
Who's there?
Shelly Cohn.
Shelly Cohn who?
Shelly Cohn carne.

Knock-knock.
Who's there?
Sherry.
Sherry who?
Sherry dance?

Knock-knock.
Who's there?
Sherwood.
Sherwood who?
Sherwood like to help you out; which way did you come in?

Knock-knock.
Who's there?
Shirley.
Shirley who?
Shirley you must know me by now.

Knock-knock.
Who's there?
Stefan.
Stefan who?
Stefan it quick before it stings me!

Knock-knock.
Who's there?
Stopwatch.
Stopwatch who?
Stopwatch you're doing this minute!

Knock-knock.
Who's there?
Stu.
Stu who?
Stu late to ask questions.

Knock-knock.
Who's there?
Sultan.
Sultan who?
Sultan pepper.

Knock-knock.
Who's there?
Summertime.
Summertime who?
Summertime you can be a big pest.

Knock-knock.
Who's there?
Sybil.
Sybil who?
"Sybil Simon met a pieman . . ."

T

Knock-knock.
Who's there?
Tad.
Tad who?
Tad's all, folks!

Knock-knock.
Who's there?
Tamara.
Tamara who?
Tamara the world.

Knock-knock.
Who's there?
Tank.
Tank who?
You're welcome.

Knock-knock.
Who's there?
Tarzan.
Tarzan who?
Tarzan stripes forever.

Knock-knock.
Who's there?
Tennis.
Tennis who?
Tennis five plus five.

Knock-knock.
Who's there?
Tex.
Tex who?
Tex two to tango.

Knock-knock.
Who's there?
Thatcher.
Thatcher who?
Thatcher could get away with it.

Knock-knock.
Who's there?
Tibet.
Tibet who?
"Early Tibet and early to rise . . ."

Knock-knock.
Who's there?
Tinker Bell.
Tinker Bell who?
Tinker Bell is out of order.

Knock-knock.
Who's there?
Tom Sawyer.
Tom Sawyer who?
Tom Sawyer underwear.

Knock-knock.
Who's there?
Arkansas.
Arkansas who?
Arkansas it, too!

Knock-knock.
Who's there?
Toby.
Toby who?
Toby or not Toby.

Knock-knock.
Who's there?
Thaddeus.
Thaddeus who?
Thaddeus question.

Knock-knock.
Who's there?
Toothy.
Toothy who?
Toothy, the day after Monday.

Knock-knock.
Wh   o's there?
Torch.
Torch who?
Torch you would never ask.

Knock-knock.
Who's there?
Toucan.
Toucan who?
Toucan live as cheaply
as one.

Knock-knock.
Who's there?
Toyota.
Toyota who?
Toyota be a law against knock-knock jokes.

Knock-knock.
Who's there?
Tuna.
Tuna who?
Tuna the radio down. It's making too much noise.

Knock-knock.
Who's there?
Turnip.
Turnip who?
Turnip the heat. It's cold out here.

Knock-knock.
Who's there?
Twig.
Twig who?
Twig or tweet!

Knock-knock.
Who's there?
Typhoid.
Typhoid who?
Typhoid that song before.

Knock-knock.
Who's there?
Tyrone.
Tyrone who?
Tyrone shoe laces.
You're big enough now.

U

Knock-knock.
Who's there?
Uganda.
Uganda who?
Uganda get away with this.

Knock-knock.
Who's there?
Uriah.
Uriah who?
Keep Uriah on
the ball.

Knock-knock.
Who's there?
Uruguay.
Uruguay who?
You go Uruguay and I'll go mine.

Knock-knock.
Who's there?
Usher.
Usher who?
Usher wish you
would let me in.

Knock-knock.
Who's there?
Uta.
Uta who?
Uta sight, uta mind.

Knock-knock.
Who's there?
Utica.
Utica who?
"Utica high road and I'll
take the low road."

V

Knock-knock.
Who's there?
Valencia.
Valencia who?
Valencia dollar, will you pay it back?

Knock-knock.
Who's there?
Value.
Value who?
Value be my Valentine?

Knock-knock.
Who's there?
Vanessa.
Vanessa who?
Vanessa you going
to grow up?

Knock-knock.
Who's there?
Vanilla.
Vanilla who?
Vanilla call the doctor.

Knock-knock.
Who's there?
Vaughan.
Vaughan who?
"Vaughan day at a time . . ."

Knock-knock.
Who's there?
Veal chop.
Veal chop who?
Veal chop for clothes tomorrow.

Knock-knock.
Who's there?
Viola.
Viola who?
Viola sudden you don't know me?

Knock-knock.
Who's there?
Violet.
Violet who?
Violet the cat out of the bag?

Knock-knock.
  Who's there?
Virtue.
  Virtue who?
Virtue get those big, brown eyes?

W

Knock-knock.
   Who's there?
Waddle.
   Waddle who?
Waddle you give me if I go away?

Knock-knock.
   Who's there?
Wafer.
   Wafer who?
Wafer a long time, but here I am again.

Knock-knock.
   Who's there?
Wah.
   Wah who?
Well, you don't have to get so excited about it!

Knock-knock.
   Who's there?
Walnuts.
   Walnuts who?
Walnuts around here.

Knock-knock.
   Who's there?
Walter.
   Walter who?
Walter-wall carpeting.

Knock-knock.
   Who's there?
Wanda.
   Wanda who?
Wanda buy some Girl Scout cookies?

Knock-knock.
   Who's there?
Wannetta.
   Wannetta who?
Wannetta time,
please.

Knock-knock.
Who's there?
Weirdo.
Weirdo who?
Weirdo you think you're going?

Knock-knock.
Who's there?
Wendy.
Wendy who?
"Wendy wind blows, the cradle will rock . . ."

Knock-knock.
Who's there?
Wheelbarrow.
Wheelbarrow who?
Wheelbarrow some money and go on a trip.

Knock-knock.
Who's there?
Whitney.
Whitney who?
Whitney have to say to me?

Knock-knock.
Who's there?
Whittle.
Whittle who?
Whittle Orphan Annie.

Knock-knock.
> *Who's there?*

Who.
> *Who who?*

You sound like an owl.

Knock-knock.
> *Who's there?*

Will you remember me in a week?
> *Yes.*

Will you remember me in a month?
> *Yes.*

Will you remember me in a year?
Yes.

Will you remember me in five years?
Yes.

Knock-knock.
> *Who's there?*

See! You've forgotten me already.

Knock-knock.
> *Who's there?*

Willis.
> *Willis who?*

Willis rain ever stop?

Knock-knock.
   Who's there?
Willoughby.
   Willoughby who?
Willoughby a monkey's uncle!

Knock-knock.
   Who's there?
Wilma.
   Wilma who?
Wilma dreams come true?

Knock-knock.
   Who's there?
Wooden shoe.
   Wooden shoe who?
Wooden shoe like to know?

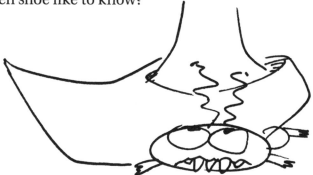

Knock-knock.
>*Who's there?*
X.
>*X who?*
X for breakfast.

Knock-knock.
>*Who's there?*
Xavier.
>*Xavier who?*
Xavier breath! I'm not leaving.

Knock-knock.
>*Who's there?*
Xenia.
>*Xenia who?*
Xenia copying my notes.

Knock-knock.
>Who's there?
Yacht.
>Yacht who?
Yacht 'a know me by now.

Knock-knock.
>Who's there?
Yah.
>Yah who?
Ride 'em, cowboy!

Knock-knock.
>Who's there?
Yelp.
>Yelp who?
Yelp me—My foot's caught in the door.

Knock-knock.
Who's there?
Yoga.
Yoga who?
Yoga what it takes!

Knock-knock.
Who's there?
Yogi Bear.
Yogi Bear who?
Yogi Bear and you're
going to get arrested.

Knock-knock.
Who's there?
Yolanda.
Yolanda who?
Yolanda me
some money?

Knock-knock.
Who's there?
You.
You who?
You who yourself!

Knock-knock.
   Who's there?
Yucatan.
   Yucatan who?
"Yucatan fool some of the people
some of the time . . ."

Knock-knock.
   Who's there?
Yucca.
   Yucca who?
"Yucca catch more flies with honey than with vinegar."

Knock-knock.
   Who's there?
Yukon.
   Yukon who?
Yukon say that again.

Knock-knock.
   Who's there?
Yvonne.
   Yvonne who?
Yvonne to
be alone?

Z

Knock-knock.
Who's there?
Zeke.
Zeke who?
"Zeke and ye shall find . . ."

Knock-knock.
Who's there?
Zinnia.
Zinnia who?
Zinnia on TV doing
an infomercial.

Knock-knock.
Who's there?
Zippy.
Zippy who?
Mrs. Zippy.

PUT~ DOWNS

10

Here Comes Trouble...

You should have been born in the Dark
Ages. You look awful in the light.

You have a striking personality.
How long has it been on strike?

You'd make a good photographer—
the way you snap at people.

I don't know what I'd do without you.
It's fun thinking about it.

Surprise me. Say
something intelligent.

Who do I think I'm
shoving? I don't know.
What's your name?

Why don't you
make like a tree
and leave?

Why don't you go to an antique store?
Maybe someone will buy you.

You have that faraway look. The farther
you get, the better you look.

You know, with the proper
amount of coaching, you
could be a nobody.

Please let me
say goodbye
until we never
meet again.

I hope you never feel
the way you look.

You'd make a
perfect stranger.

You don't know the meaning of the word
fear. You're too scared to look it up.

You're not yourself today. I noticed
the improvement right away.

I admit that you're stronger than I am, but bad breath isn't everything.

You're so weak, you couldn't bend a wet noodle.

You're so weak, you couldn't even crack a joke.

You're in such bad shape, you couldn't jump to a conclusion.

You're such a coward, you're afraid to strike a bargain.

You're such a coward, you won't even strike a match.

Two's company. You're a crowd.

Want to see something funny? Look in the mirror.

11

Things Could Be Worse

Things could be worse.
You could be here in person.

How long can a person live without
a brain? How old are you?

I believe in the hereafter—
so hereafter, don't bother me.

Some people bring happiness wherever they
go; you bring happiness whenever you go.

Tell me about yourself.
I enjoy horror stories.

When you come into a room,
the mice jump on a chair.

It takes all kinds of people
to make up the world.
Too bad you're not one of them.

If you tried to join the
human race, you'd be
turned down.

You must be a tolerant person.
How else could you stand yourself?

As an outsider, what do you
think of the human race?

You're such a sourpuss, when you suck a
lemon—the lemon makes faces.

The closest you'll ever get to being
brave is to eat a hero sandwich.

They should cover you with
chocolate, because you're nuts!

Do you have a
license to drive
people crazy?

Have you been to the zoo
lately? I mean, as a visitor?

The only thing
that you can keep
in your head for
more than an
hour is a cold.

You hold your nose so high in the air, there's always an inch of snow on it.

Some people are born great, some achieve greatness—you just grate.

You ought to be an auto racer— you're such a big drag.

Whatever is eating you must be suffering from indigestion.

12

All Right, Let'S Hear It!

You must have
a clean mind—
you change
it so often.

You never change your mind?
No wonder—no mind.

Who wears your good clothes?

I don't believe in talking to strangers—
and you're the strangest person I ever saw.

You say you have a mind of your own? Why
don't you bring it around some time?

Do it tomorrow. You've made
enough mistakes today.

Your idea of a big evening is to
take out the garbage.

Of course I'm listening to you.
Don't you see me yawning?

I've heard so much about you.
What's your side of the story?

How many rocks did they
have to turn up before
you crawled out?

You're the kind of person
who lights up a room
by leaving it.

I don't know what's bothering
you, but I hope it isn't catching.

I thought my razor was dull
until I heard you talk.

I liked the song you sang.
One day you should put it to music.

The next time you get a toupee,
get one with brains.

You're all wrapped up
in yourself—
and you make a
pretty small package.

You think you're a
big cheese—but you
only smell like one.

You could make a
fortune renting out
your head as a balloon.

If they're not talking about you,
you're not listening.

13

Happy
Valentine's Day

How much would it cost to buy back
my introduction to you?

You're neither right-handed
nor left-handed—just
under-handed.

The only prints you'll
leave on the sands of
time will be heel marks.

Would you mind reaching into your heart
and getting me a piece of ice?

You may think you're a bookworm,
but you're only the ordinary kind.

Tell me, if I gave you two aspirins,
would you go away?

I'd like to say hello to you
so that I can say goodbye
to you.

Let's play Building and Loan.
Get out of the building and
leave me alone.

I'll forgive your rudeness—
I know you're just being yourself.

You're definitely
non habit-forming.

If you ever need a friend—
buy a dog.

The only way you'll
ever get polish is to
drink it.

You must be a magician. You can turn
anything into an argument.

There are going to be a lot of empty
seats at your testimonial dinner.

I'll say one thing for you: you have
an even disposition—always mean.

Why don't you take a long
walk off a short pier?

Don't think—you could
strain yourself.

I like your approach. Now, let's see your departure.

Keep your temper. I don't want it.

You really work hard at being difficult, don't you?

Make like a snake and slither away!

14

Tooth & Consequences

You may become famous in history—medical history!

Whatever is eating you must be suffering from food poisoning.

When your grandfather was born, they passed out cigars. When your father was born, they passed out cigarettes. When you were born, they just passed out.

When you were born, your parents looked up your birth certificate to see if there were any loopholes in it.

You're a chip off the old block— a real blockhead.

You're just what the doctor ordered—a pill!

Your remarks may be pointless, but not your head.

Stay with me—
I want to be alone.

Why don't you make like
dandruff and flake off?

You're in fantastic condition.
In fact, I never saw anyone in
your condition.

Did you fill in that
blank yet? I mean the one
between your ears.

Your clothes look pretty good
considering the shape they're on.

You remind me of the
Liberty Bell—cracked.

The softness of your
muscles is only
exceeded by the
hardness of your head.

If you went to a mind reader,
you'd only be charged half-price.

Even people who don't know you don't like you.

Why don't you leave your
brain to science? Maybe they
can find a cure for it.

Most of us live and learn; you just live.

I've got something in my eye that's painful—you.

Beauty isn't everything. In
your case, it's nothing.

Please make like a ball and roll away!

If you need me—hesitate to call.

15
Karate Chops

"I'm a self-made man."
   "I accept your apology."

"Where do you bathe?"
   "In the spring."
"I didn't ask you when, I asked you where."

                    "You must be a terrific bowler."
                       "How did you know?"
                    "I could tell by your pin head."

"What's your name?"
   "Pistachio."
"Pistachio! What kind
of name is that?"
   *"That's Pistachio
   to my friends—
   and nuts to you!"*

"Singers run in my family."
"They should."

"Only fools make absolute statements."
"Are you sure of that?"
"Absolutely!"

"Would you like to travel to unknown places?"
"Yes, I would."
"Fine, go get lost."

16
Hey, Waiter!

CUSTOMER: Waiter, there's a fly in my soup!

WAITER: *Don't worry, sir, the spider on the bread will take care of it.*

CUSTOMER: Say, waiter, why do you have your thumb on my steak?

WAITER: *I don't want it to fall on the floor again.*

CUSTOMER: Do you serve crabs here?

WAITER: *We serve everyone. Sit right down.*

CUSTOMER: I feel like a sandwich.
WAITER: *Funny, you don't look like one.*

CUSTOMER: This soup isn't fit for a pig!
WAITER: *I'll take it back, sir, and bring you some that is.*

CUSTOMER: There's a fly in my soup!
WAITER: *What do you expect me to do—hold a funeral?*

"You look full."
"How full?"
"Aw-ful."

CUSTOMER: Waiter, how come this sandwich is squashed?
WAITER: *You told me to step on it, didn't you?*

"Waiter!"
"Yes, sir?"
"What's this?"
"It's bean soup, sir."
"I don't want to know what it's been—what is it now?"

CUSTOMER: Hey, waiter! What kind of pie did you bring me? Are you sure this is apple pie?
WAITER: *What does it taste like?*
CUSTOMER: I don't know.
WAITER: *Then what difference does it make?*

WAITER: I have boiled tongue, fried liver, and pig's feet.
CUSTOMER: *I'm not interested in your medical problems. Just bring me a cheese sandwich and coffee.*

CUSTOMER: Waiter, do you have frog's legs?
WAITER: *Yes, sir.*
CUSTOMER: Then why don't you hop into the kitchen and get me a doughnut and coffee?

CUSTOMER: Do you have pig's feet?
WAITER: *Yes, I do.*
CUSTOMER: Too bad.
    If you wear shoes, maybe no one will notice.

CUSTOMER: May I have a glass of water?
WAITER: *To drink?*
CUSTOMER: No, I want to rinse out a few things.

CUSTOMER: What's the difference between the blue-plate
    and the white-plate special?
WAITER: *The white-plate special is ten cents extra.*
CUSTOMER: Is the food any better?
WAITER: *No, but we wash the dishes.*

WAITER: Is the food too spicy?
CUSTOMER: *Not at all. Smoke always comes
    out of my ears.*

WAITER: Oh, I'm
    sorry I spilled
    water all over
    you.
CUSTOMER: *That's all
    right. My suit was
    several sizes too
    large, anyhow.*

CUSTOMER: I'm giving a dinner
    for all my friends tonight.
WAITER: *Oh—you must be the
    party that reserved a table
    for two.*

CUSTOMER: May I have a glass of water, please?
WAITER: *To drink?*
CUSTOMER: No—to do a high diving act.

CUSTOMER: I understand that fish is brain food.
WAITER: *Yes, I eat it all the time.*
CUSTOMER: Oh, well, there goes another scientific theory.

CUSTOMER: I have a complaint.
WAITER: *A complaint! This is a restaurant— not a hospital.*

17
Exercising with Dumbbells

"Would you join me in a walk?"
    "I'd love to."
"Good. My doctor told me to exercise with dumbbells."

"Haven't I seen your face somewhere else?"
    "I don't think so. It's always been between my ears."

Just because you've been off base all your life doesn't make you a baseball player.

If your head was an automobile gas tank, it would point to empty.

Signal me when you've finished talking so I can take my fingers out of my ears.

Why don't you introduce your mind to your mouth?

What does your brain want to be when it grows up?

"Do you know the difference between a piece of birthday cake and an old glove?"

"*No.*"

"Good, then eat this old glove."

The closest you'll ever come to a brainstorm is a light drizzle.

It gives me a headache just to think down to your level.

"If I stand on my head, all my blood rushes into it. Why doesn't all my blood rush to my feet when I stand on them?"

"*Your feet aren't empty.*"

You're in such bad shape, you get winded playing chess!

I hear you tried to join the human race but flunked the physical.

18

I'm Speechless!

"I'm speechless!"
  "If only you'd stay that way!"

"I heard about your wit."
 "Oh, it's nothing."
"Yes—that's what I heard."

"When I got up on that stage, people clapped their hands."
  "Yes, over their eyes."

ACTOR: Have you seen me on television?
ACQUAINTANCE: *On and off.*
ACTOR: How did you like me?
ACQUAINTANCE: *Off.*

"That play I was in had a happy ending."
 "Yes, everyone was glad it was over."

"People say you're so conceited you write letters to yourself."
 "Dear me!"
"Yes—that's how they begin."

"What would you say if I asked you to marry me?"
"Nothing. I can't talk and laugh at the same time."

"Have you told your little boy not to go around imitating me?"
"Yes, I have. I told him not to act like an idiot."

"You should put a sign on your head."
"What kind of sign?"
"VACANT."

"I learned to play the piano in no time."
"Yes, and you play it that way, too."

"I've been playing the piano for five years."
"Aren't your fingers tired?"

"You're half an hour late. I've been standing here like a fool."
"I can't help how you stand."

"How are you?"
"Wonderful."
"I'm glad someone thinks so."

The more I think of you—the less I think of you.

Your problem is that you're always trying to save both faces.

"I can't get to sleep at night. I've tried all kinds of remedies, but nothing works."
"Have you tried talking to yourself?"

You have an even disposition—always rotten.

"Before I do anything, I stop to think."
"The trouble is you always forget to start again."

"Am I boring you?"
"No, just wake me when you're finished."

"If you work hard, you'll get ahead."
"No, thanks, I already have a head."

My house is located near a lake. Drop in some time.

JOKES

19

Quickies

Advice to worms: Sleep late!

Did you hear about the cannibal who liked to stop where they serve truck drivers?

DOORMAN: Your car is at the door, sir.
CAR OWNER: *Yes, I hear it knocking.*

FLIP: Do you live in a small house?
FLOP: *Small! Ours is the only house in town with round-shouldered mice.*

PATIENT: Doctor, will you treat me?
DOCTOR: *Absolutely not! You'll have to pay the same as everyone else.*

SILLY: What did the police do when two hundred hares escaped from the rabbit farm?

SILLIER: *They combed the area.*

There's a new book out called *How to Be Happy without Money.* It costs ten dollars.

Sign on a cleaning store specializing in gloves:

WE CLEAN YOUR DIRTY KIDS

One skeleton to the other: "If we had any guts, we'd get out of here."

FATHER TO SON: I don't care if the basement wall is cracking. Please stop telling everyone you come from a broken home.

Did you hear about the snake charmer who married an undertaker? They now have towels marked "Hiss" and "Hearse."

FLIP: If you were in a jungle by yourself and an elephant charged you, what would you do?
FLOP: *Pay him.*

"Hello, operator, I'd like to speak to the king of the jungle."
"I'm very sorry, but the lion is busy."

Advertisement:
FOR SALE: LARGE CRYSTAL VASE BY LADY SLIGHTLY CRACKED.

My dog likes to eat garlic. Now his bark is *much* worse than his bite.

They laughed when they saw me sit down at the piano with both hands tied behind my back. They didn't know I played by ear.

You'll be revered one day, Paul.

I don't give a fig about you, Newton.

MOTHER MONSTER TO LITTLE SON: Please don't set in that chair! We're saving it for Rigor Mortis to set in.

Sign outside a restaurant:
DON'T STAND OUTSIDE AND BE MISERABLE— COME INSIDE AND BE FED UP.

My cellar is so damp, when I lay a mousetrap, I catch fish.

NIP: The garbage man is here.
TUCK: *Tell him we don't want any.*

Sign in a restaurant window:
EAT NOW—PAY WAITER.

TEACHER: Spell Tennessee, Johnny.
JOHNNY: *One-a-see, two-a-see . . .*

Hot weather never bothers me.
I just throw the thermometer out
of the window and watch the
temperature drop.

Every time I get
on a ferry it makes
me cross.

I was teacher's pet.
She couldn't afford a dog.

Wise man says:

The bigger the summer vacation,
the harder the fall.

Old refrigerators never die,
they just lose their cool.

Show me a dog in the middle of a muddy road,
and I'll show you a mutt in a rut.

Show me a pink polka-dot pony,
and I'll show you a horse of a different color.

Show me a thirsty tailor
and I'll show you a dry cleaner.

TEACHER: Joseph, name two pronouns.
JOSEPH: *Who, me?*
TEACHER: Correct!

CLARA: Do you realize it takes
    three sheep to make one sweater?
SARAH: *I didn't even know*
    they could knit.

My dog is a terrible bloodhound.
I cut my hand once and he fainted.

ERNIE: Does your dog have a license?
BERNIE: *No, she's not old enough to drive.*

Wise man says:

When in doubt, mumble.

NIT: Blood is thicker than water.
WIT: So is toothpaste.

The study of language can be ridiculous sometimes.
I heard of someone who is beginning Finnish.

He didn't know the meaning of the
word "fear." (He was too afraid to ask.)

To WAITER: Who made this Caesar salad—Brutus?

Did you hear about the
hippie who starved to death
rather than have a square
meal?

"Waiter, please get that fly out of my soup.
I want to dine alone."

Why don't you go to a tailor and have a fit!

There's a scale over there. Go weigh!

Why don't you learn to play the guitar
and stop picking on me?

FLAP: Hello, old top! New car?
JACK: *No, old car. New top.*

TAXI DRIVER: Look outside and see if my
blinker is on.
PASSENGER: *Yes-no-yes-no-yes-no.*

Sign in car wrecker's lot:
RUST IN PEACE.

Did you hear about the elephant who went to the beach to
see something new in trunks?

DOCTOR: How did you get here so fast?
PATIENT: *Flu.*

PATIENT: What does the X ray of my head show?
DOCTOR: *Nothing.*

"I told you not to swallow!" yelled the dentist. "That was my last pair of pliers."

Are you a man or a mouse?
Squeak up!

He's so weak, when he tries to whip cream, the cream wins.

WAITER: These are the best eggs we've had for years.
CUSTOMER: *Well, bring me some you haven't had around for that long.*

DOCTOR: Did you take the patient's temperature?
NURSE: *No, is it missing?*

NITA: I lived for a week on a can of sardines.
RITA: *How did you keep from falling off?*

If the world is getting smaller, how come they keep raising the postal rates?

CUSTOMER: Waiter, bring me some turtle soup and make it snappy!

WAITER (TO CUSTOMER): Don't complain about the coffee. You may be old and weak yourself some day.

"Will you pass the nuts, teacher?"
"No. I think I'll flunk them."

20 Crazies

PATIENT: *Doctor, you must help me.*
I can't remember anything.
DOCTOR: How long has this been going on?
PATIENT: *How long has what been going on?*

CUSTOMER: Waiter, are you sure this ham
was cured?
WAITER: *Certainly, sir.*
CUSTOMER: From its taste, I would say it's
still sick.

CUSTOMER: Waiter, what kind of soup is this? I
ordered pea soup, this tastes like soap.
WAITER: *My mistake, that's tomato soup. Pea soup*
tastes like gasoline.

SAM: I'm having a lot of trouble with eczema, teacher.

TEACHER: *Heavens, where do you have it?*

SAM: I don't have it, I just can't spell it.

An excited woman telephoned her doctor, "Doctor, doctor, my husband swallowed a mouse! What shall I do?

"Wave a piece of cheese in front of his mouth until I get there," the doctor said.

Fifteen minutes later he arrived at the house to find the woman waving a sardine in front of her husband's mouth.

"I said a piece of cheese, not a sardine!" exclaimed the doctor.

"I know you did," the woman replied, "But I have to get the cat out first."

FARMER: On my farm we go to bed with the chickens.

CITY SLICKER: *In the city, we'd rather sleep in our own beds.*

CUSTOMER (AT NUT COUNTER): Who's in charge of the nuts around here?

CLERK: *One moment, please, and I'll take care of you.*

A city man was driving in the country when he took the wrong turn and got lost. He drove down a dirt road, hoping to find someone who might help him. He came to a fork in the road but couldn't decide which turn to take. Then he spotted a man rocking on a porch nearby.

"Hey, there!" he shouted. "Can you tell me where the road on the left leads to?"

"Don't rightly know," the man replied, continuing to rock.

"Well, can you tell me where the road on the right leads to?"

Again, the man on the porch said he didn't know.

The motorist became angry. "You're not very bright, are you?" he shouted.

"Maybe not," the man replied calmly, "but I'm not lost."

DOCTOR: What's the trouble?

PATIENT: *I think I'm a dog.*

DOCTOR: How long has this been going on?

PATIENT: *Ever since I was a puppy.*

PSYCHIATRIST: What's your problem?

PATIENT: *I prefer bow ties to long ties.*

PSYCHIATRIST: Is that all? Thousands of people prefer bow ties. In fact, so do I.

PATIENT: *You do? What a relief! How do you like yours, boiled or fried?*

Did you hear about the banker who could no longer ride a bike because he lost his balance?

"I don't care who you are, get your reindeer off my roof!"

TEACHER: How much is half of 8?

SUZIE: *Up and down or across?*

TEACHER: What do you mean?

SUZIE: *Up and down it's 3, and across it's 0.*

A deep-sea diver had just reached the bottom when an urgent message came from the surface: "Come up quickly— the ship is sinking!"

JOHN (OFFERING CHOCOLATE): Here, honey, sweets to the sweet.

MARY: *Oh, thank you! Won't you have some of these nuts?*

TEACHER: Can anyone name a deadly poison?

PUPIL: *Aviation!*

TEACHER: Aviation?

PUPIL: *Sure. One drop and you're dead.*

CUSTOMER: Waiter, there's a button in my salad. I want to see the manager!

WAITER: *Don't get so excited. It probably fell off while the salad was dressing.*

CUSTOMER: What dishes do you have for me to eat?

WAITER (IN A HORRIFIED VOICE): *You eat dishes?*

WOMAN: Doctor, please come quickly! My little boy has just swallowed a fountain pen.

DOCTOR: *Of course, I'll be right there. What are you doing in the meantime?*

WOMAN: Using a pencil.

Three men were sitting on a park bench. The man in the middle was reading a newspaper. The two men on either side were going through the motions as if they were actually fishing. They carefully baited their hooks, cast out the line, and reeled them in when they had an imaginary bite.

A policeman stopped when he saw what was going on. Puzzled, he asked the man in the middle if he knew the two men on either side. The man folded his newspaper and admitted they were his friends.

"In that case," warned the policeman, "you'd better get them out of here!"

"Yes, officer!" the man replied, as he began to row furiously.

A motorist, traveling in backwoods country, found the bridge over a stream washed away. He noticed a man sitting nearby whittling away at a stick.

"How deep is the stream?" the motorist asked.

"Not too deep," the man replied.

"Think I can drive through it?" the motorist asked.

"I reckon you can," the man replied.

Hearing this, the motorist got into his car and started across the stream. However, the car sank in the middle of the stream and the motorist barely escaped with his life.

"What do you mean by telling me I could drive across?" said he asked angrily. "That stream is at least ten feet deep."

The man whittling scratched his head. "Funny," he said, "it only reaches up to the middle of the ducks."

Cannibal chief's wife to a friend: "Be sure to drop in Friday night. We're having the Joneses for dinner."

JUNIOR: I'm so glad you named me Joe.
MOTHER: *Why do you say that?*
JUNIOR: Because that's what all the kids in school call me.

JOE: Do you still walk in your sleep?
MOE: *Not any more. Now I take carfare with me when I go to bed.*

CUSTOMER: Waiter, I'm hungry. Please bring me a mashed potato sandwich on rye.

WAITER: *What are you saying? Only an idiot would order mashed potatoes on rye bread.*

CUSTOMER: You're right. Make it on whole wheat toast.

CUSTOMER: Waiter, would you please put the rest of my steak into a doggie bag?

WAITER: *Certainly. Anything else?*

CUSTOMER: Better put some bread and butter in it too, in case my dog wants to make a sandwich.

CUSTOMER: There's something wrong with these hot dogs.

WAITER: *Sorry, sir, I can't help you. I'm a waiter, not a veterinarian.*

TEACHER: If I write *n-e-w* on the blackboard, what does that spell?

SAMMY: *New.*

TEACHER: Correct. Now if I put a "k" in front of it, what have we now?

SAMMY: *Canoe?*

Sign at a garden center:

PLANT OUR SEEDS AND JUMP BACK!

Monkey Business

JUNIOR: Mom, how much am I worth?

MOTHER: *To me, dear, you're worth all the money in the world.*

JUNIOR: In that case, can I have a quarter?

BANKER: You can't open an account with this kind of money. These are wooden nickels!

LUMBERJACK: *That's all right. I only want to open a shavings account.*

BIFF: Lend me ten dollars.

BOFF: *I can't spare it.*

BIFF: All right, lend me ten dollars and give me five dollars now. Then I'll owe you five dollars, and you'll owe me five dollars, and we'll call it square.

MIKE: Lend me fifty dollars.

MMIKE: *I only have forty.*

MIKE: Well then, let me have the forty, and you can owe me the other ten.

CUSTOMER: Waiter, this food gives me heartburn.

WAITER: *What did you expect—sunburn?*

Book Club Selections

How to Lead a Parade by Marcia Long

Exercise for Pleasure by Charlie Haws

American Patriotic Songs by Orlando D. Free and Homer D. Brave

Monster Making as a Hobby by Frank N. Stine

Arithmetic Simplified by Lois Carmen Denominator

Favorite Breakfast Recipes by Hammond Ecks

I Was a Door-to-Door Salesman by Belle Ringer

How to Apologize by Thayer Thorry

Guide to Justice by Dolores Clear

What's Up, Doc? by Howie Dewin

Stories from the Insane Asylum by I. M. Nutty

SHOPPER: What's the price of hamburger meat?

BUTCHER: *Ninety cents a pound.*

SHOPPER: Ninety cents a pound! But the store down the street sells it for sixty cents a pound.

BUTCHER: *Why don't you go there to shop?*

SHOPPER: *I did, but they're out of it.*

BUTCHER: Well, when I am out of hamburger, I sell it for *forty* cents a pound.

The country needed more money, so it opened a new mint which operates from 7 P.M. to midnight. This makes it the world's largest after-dinner mint.

KNIGHT: I bought this suit here two weeks ago and it looks rusty already.

ARMOR MAKER: *Well, I said it would wear like iron, didn't I?*

SNIP: I went window shopping today.
SNAP: *Did you get anything?*
SNIP: Yes, I bought four windows.

DIT: Where did Larry go?
DOT: *He's round in front.*
DIT: I know what he looks like, I just wanted to know where he went.

A woman opened her refrigerator door and found a rabbit inside.

"What are you doing in my refrigerator?" she asked.

"Isn't this a Westinghouse?" the rabbit wanted to know.

"Yes," said the woman.

"Well," replied the rabbit, "I'm westing."

Sign in a real estate office:

LOTS FOR LITTLE

REAL ESTATE AGENT: Here is a house without a flaw.
CUSTOMER: *My goodness, what do you walk on?*

DIT: Speaking of inflation, have you any idea of the price of feather pillows these days?
DOT: *Not really.*
DIT: Why, even down is up.

POLICEMAN: Hey, you! You're crossing the street when the light says Don't Walk.
PEDESTRIAN: *Sorry, officer, I thought that was an ad for the bus company.*

NIT: How did you manage to pass the geometry test without studying?
WIT: *I knew all the angles.*

TEACHER: Where is your pencil, Harold?
HAROLD: *I ain't got none.*
TEACHER: How many times have I told you not to say that, Harold? Now listen: I do not have a pencil, you do not have a pencil, they do not have a pencil. Now, Harold, do you understand?
HAROLD: *Not really. What happened to all the pencils?*

A gorilla walked up to a soda fountain and ordered a chocolate ice cream soda. The man behind the counter was amazed to hear the gorilla speak, but he brought the ice cream soda anyway.

The gorilla finished the ice cream soda and handed the man a ten dollar bill. The man did not believe the gorilla knew anything about money, so he only gave back one dollar in change.

"Hope you enjoyed the soda," he said to the gorilla. "We don't get too many gorillas coming in here."

"At nine dollars a soda," said the gorilla, "it's no wonder."

"So, you run a duck farm," said the city visitor. "Is business picking up?"

"No, picking down," replied the farmer.

The farmer came into the bank and asked the guard who arranges for loans.

"I'm sorry, sir," the guard told him, "but the loan arranger is out to lunch."

"All right," the farmer said, "can I speak to Tonto?"

Sign at a butcher shop:

**HONEST SCALES—
NO TWO WEIGHS ABOUT IT**

Sign in funeral parlor:

**SATISFACTION GUARANTEED
OR YOUR MUMMY BACK**

Sign on a travel agency window:

PLEASE GO AWAY!

Sign on a canary cage in a pet shop:

FOR SALE—CHEEP

Sign at a tire store:

WE SKID YOU NOT

Have you heard about the new Christmas gift item? It's a combination record player and air conditioner—for people who like to play it cool.

Sign on a tailor shop:

**WE'LL CLEAN FOR YOU.
WE'LL PRESS FOR YOU.
WE'LL EVEN DYE FOR YOU!**

Sign in a shoe store window:

COME IN AND HAVE A FIT

ANGRY BUYER: This car won't go up hills and you said it was a fine machine.

AUTO DEALER: *I said, "On the level, it's a fine machine."*

CLIENT: I'll give you $500 if you do the worrying for me.

LAWYER: *Fine. Now where is the $500?*

CLIENT: That is your first worry.

Advertisement:

WANTED: HOTEL WORKERS.
ONLY INN-EXPERIENCED NEED APPLY.

Sign on a garbage truck:

SATISFACTION GUARANTEED—
OR DOUBLE YOUR GARBAGE BACK

LEM: Down on our farm, we had a hen lay an egg six inches long.

CLEM: *That's nothing much. On our farm we can beat that.*

LEM: How?

CLEM: *With an egg beater.*

TEACHER: What's a conductor of electricity?

LOUELLA: *Why, er-r—*

TEACHER: Correct. Now tell me, Louella, what is the unit of electric power?

LOUELLA: *The "what"?*

TEACHER: Correct, very good.

CUSTOMER: Waiter! There's no turtle in the turtle soup.

WAITER: *Of course. If you look close you'll see that there's also no horse in the horseradish.*

CUSTOMER: Waiter, this soup tastes funny.

WAITER: *Then why aren't you laughing?*

ERNIE: To the right of me was a ferocious lion, on my left a tiger ready to spring, and in back and in front of me were stampeding elephants!

BERNIE: *How did you escape?*

ERNIE: I got off the merry-go-round.

Oldies but Goodies

Two hillbillies were fishing. For three hours neither of them moved a muscle. Then one became restless. His companion grumbled, "That's the second time you've moved your feet in twenty minutes. Did you come here to fish or to dance?"

IGGY: Did you take a bath today?
ZIGGY. *Why? Is one missing?*

LITTLE SUZIE: Mother, you know that vase you said had been handed down from generation to generation?
MOTHER: *Yes.*
LITTLE SUZIE: Well, this generation just dropped it.

PILOT: Do you wanna' fly?

CO-PILOT: *Sure.*

PILOT: Wait a second and I'll catch one for you.

DIT: Did you hear about the delicatessen that kept bandages in the refrigerator?

DOT: *Whatever for?*

DIT: For cold cuts.

Did you hear about the bank clerk who climbed a tree because he wanted to become a branch manager?

Wise man says:

Those who eat sweets—take up two seats.

Did you hear about the mad scientist who invented a square bathtub so it never left a ring?

"He was a Marine corporal, but they had to kick him out."

   "What for?"

"Because he was rotten to the Corps."

JULIET: Romeo, O Romeo, wherefore art thou?

ROMEO: *Down here in the flowers. The trellis broke.*

NIT: No one can stop time, they say.
WIT: *I don't know. Why, just this morning I saw a policeman go into a store and stop a few minutes.*

FLO: What's the name of your dog?
MOE: *Ginger.*
FLO: Does Ginger bite?
MOE: *No, but Ginger snaps.*

PITTER: I have a three-season bed.
PAT: *What's a three-season bed?*
PITTER: One without a spring.

CUSTOMER: Waiter, there's a fly in my soup.
WAITER: *How much can a little fly drink?*

CUSTOMER: Waiter, what's this fly doing in my soup?
WAITER: *It looks like the backstroke to me.*

CUSTOMER: There's a fly in my soup.
WAITER: *Well, it's better than having no meat at all.*

BIG AL: What are you doing with a pencil and paper?
LITTLE AL: *I'm writing a letter to my brother.*
BIG AL: But you don't know how to write.
LITTLE AL: *That's okay, my brother can't read.*

ERNIE: What's your pet pig's name?
BERNIE: *Ballpoint.*
ERNIE: Is that his real name?
BERNIE: *No, that's his pen name.*

GOODENOV: I woke up last night with the feeling that my watch was gone. So I looked for it.
BADENOV: *Was it gone?*
GOODENOV: No, but it was going.

JUDGE: Driving through a red light will cost you $25 and costs, and next time you go to jail. Is that clear?
DRIVER: *Yes, your honor. Just like a weather report—fine today, cooler tomorrow.*

MOTHER: Who gave you the black eye?
BOY: *Nobody. I had to fight for it.*

MOTHER: Now, Junior, eat your spinach.
  It's good for growing children.
JUNIOR: *Who wants to grow children?*

Wise man says:

  Many a true word is spoken through false teeth.

FATHER: How did you do in your exams today, Junior?

JUNIOR: *I did what George Washington did.*

FATHER: What was that?

JUNIOR: *I went down in history.*

TEACHER: What does it mean when the barometer is falling?

PUPIL: *It means that whoever nailed it up didn't do such a good job.*

FLIP: How were the exam questions?

FLOP: *Easy.*

FLIP: Then why do you look so unhappy?

FLOP: *The questions didn't give me any trouble—just the answers.*

TEACHER: Order, children, order!

SAMMY: *I'll have a hamburger and a soda, please.*

A pet store owner was trying to sell a dog to a customer. It was a hot day and the dog was breathing hard with his long tongue hanging out.

"Don't you admire his coat?" the store owner asked.

"Coat's all right," the customer replied, "but I don't care for the pants."

A woman nodded to the minister as he passed. "Mother," asked Junior, "who was that man?"

"That is the man who married me," Mother replied.

"If that is the man who married you," asked Junior, "what's Daddy doing in our house?"

DICK: Great news! Teacher said we would have a test today, rain or shine.
JANE: *What's so great about that?*
DICK: It's snowing.

NED: I know someone who whistles while he works.
TED: *Is he that happy?*
NED: No, he's a traffic policeman.

AUZIE: Mother, I can't go to school today.
MOTHER: *Why not?*
AUZIE: I don't feel well.
MOTHER: *Where don't you feel well?*
AUZIE: In school.

23

Unfriendly Advice

A child was making a nuisance of himself by playing ball in the aisle of an airplane. One man was particularly annoyed and finally lost his temper.

"Listen, kid," he said. "Why don't you go outside and play?"

Sign on newly seeded lawn:

DOGS BEWARE, VICIOUS MAN!

PATIENT: Doctor, I get the feeling that people don't give a hoot about anything I say.
PSYCHIATRIST: *So?*

MOTHER (ON PHONE): Doctor, doctor! Junior has swallowed a bullet. What should I do?

DOCTOR: *Don't point him at anybody.*

DOCTOR: What's the problem?

PATIENT: *I swallowed a roll of film.*

DOCTOR: Don't worry, nothing serious will develop.

Three boys walked into a candy store. The first one said, "I want a dime's worth of jelly beans."

It happened that the jelly beans were way up on the top shelf. The old storekeeper had to get a ladder and climb up, bring down the jar, count out ten cents worth of jelly beans, climb up and put the jar back. Then the storekeeper climbed down, put the ladder away and turned to the second boy.

"I want a dime's worth of jelly beans, too," said the boy.

So the old man got the ladder, climbed up and brought down the jar, counted out another dime's worth of jelly beans. However, before he put the jar back, he had a thought. He said to the third boy: "Do you want a dime's worth of jelly beans, too?

"No," the boy replied.

So the old man climbed up, returned the jar, climbed down, put the ladder away, and came back to the counter.

"Now," he said to the third boy, "what can I do for you?"

"I want a nickel's worth of jelly beans."

TEACHER: Sam, what's the outside of a tree called?

SAM: *I don't know.*

TEACHER: Bark, Sam, bark.

SAM: *Bow wow wow!*

"Mommy, all the kids say I look like a werewolf."

"*Shut up and comb your face!*"

CUSTOMER: Waiter, there's a fly in this ice cream.

WAITER: *Serves him right. Let him freeze!*

Slavemaster to Roman galley slaves who have been pulling on oars for hours:

I have some good news for you and some bad news. The good news is: you can have fifteen minutes' rest. Now for the bad news: At the end of the rest period, the captain wants to go water-skiing.

FIRST RANCHER: What's the name of your place?
SECOND RANCHER: *The XWK Lazy R Double Diamond Circle Q Bar S.*
FIRST RANCHER: How many head of cattle do you have?
SECOND RANCHER: *Only a few. Not many survive the branding.*

DOCTOR: Ouch! OUCH!
MOTHER: *Junior, please say "ah" so the nice doctor can take his finger out of your mouth.*

MOTHER: How do you like your new teacher?
LITTLE GIRL: *I don't like her very much.*
MOTHER: Why not?
LITTLE GIRL: *She told me to sit up front for the present—and then she didn't give me a present.*

FATHER: Junior, I see by your report card that you're not doing well in history. How come?
JUNIOR: *I can't help it. The teacher always asks me about things that happened before I was born.*

TEACHER: Why are you crawling into class, Arthur?
ARTHUR: *Because class has already started and you said, "Don't walk into my class late!"*

DOCTOR: How do you feel today?
PATIENT: *Very much better, thank you. The only thing still bothering me is my breathing.*
DOCTOR: We'll try to find something to stop that.

HORACE: That is a beautiful stuffed lion you have there. Where did you get him?
MORRIS: *In Africa, when I was on a hunting expedition with my uncle.*
HORACE: What's he stuffed with?
MORRIS: *My uncle.*

TIP: Did I ever tell you the story about my forebears?
TOP: *No, but I've heard the one about the three bears.*

Sign in a pet shop window:

BOXER PUPPY FOR SALE. HOUSEBROKEN, FAITHFUL, WILL EAT ANYTHING. ESPECIALLY FOND OF CHILDREN.

FIRST INVISIBLE MAN: Did you miss me when I was gone?
SECOND INVISIBLE MAN: *Were you gone?*

IGOR: You remind me of a pie.
BORIS: *You mean I'm sweet?*
IGOR: No, you have some crust.

HUSBAND: My hair is getting thinner.
WIFE: *So what? Who wants fat hair?*

TEACHER: Let us take the example of the busy ant. He works
all the time, night and day. Then what happens?
PUPIL: *He gets stepped on.*

TUTTI: There was once a lord who owned many castles.
When he gave them up, he became very rude.
FRUTTI: *Would you say he lost all his manors?*

The dentist walked up to his patient, who let out a wild scream.

"What are you hollering for?" the dentist asked. "You're not even in the chair yet."

"I know, Doc," the patient answered, "but you're stepping on my foot."

NED: I just burned a hundred dollar bill.
FRED: *Wow! You must be rich.*
NED: Not really. It was a bill from my dentist.

A family that had spent its vacation on a farm the year before wished to return again. The only thing wrong with the farm was the noise the pigs made.

The family wrote to the farmer to ask if the pigs were still there. The farmer wrote back, "Don't worry. We haven't had pigs on the farm since you were here."

HARRY: Didn't you say your dog's bark was worse than his bite?
LARRY: *Yes I did.*
HARRY: Then for goodness sake, don't let him bark. He just bit me.

LEM: Don't be afraid. This dog will eat off your hand.

CLEM: *That's exactly what I'm afraid of.*

JUNIOR: Is it true we are made of dust, Mummy?

MOTHER: *Yes, dear.*

JUNIOR: Is it true we turn back to dust when we die?

MOTHER: *That's what the Bible says.*

JUNIOR: Well, Mummy, I just looked under my bed and someone's either coming or going.

A horse walked into a soda fountain and ordered an ice cream sundae with chocolate ice cream and strawberry syrup, sprinkled with nuts.

The young man behind the counter brought the sundae to the horse, who finished it off with great pleasure.

Noticing how the young man stared at him as he ate, the horse said, "I suppose you think it strange that a horse should come into a soda fountain and order a sundae with chocolate ice cream and strawberry syrup, sprinkled with nuts?"

"Not at all," the young man replied. "I like it that way myself."

IRV: What are you up to?

MERV: *I'm writing a letter to myself.*

IRV: What does it say?

MERV: *I don't know. I won't get it until tomorrow.*

NITA: The trouble with you is you're always wishing for something you don't have.

RITA: *Well, what else is there to wish for?*

LEM: Did you hear about the turtle on the New Jersey Turnpike?

CLEM: *What was the turtle doing on the turnpike?*

LEM: About one mile an hour.

TEACHER (CORRECTING A PUPIL): When I asked you what shape the world was in, I meant "round" or "flat"—not "rotten."

FIRST MOUSE: I finally got that scientist trained.

SECOND MOUSE: *How so?*

FIRST MOUSE: Every time I go through that maze and ring the bell, he gives me something to eat.

TEACHER: If you add 3,462 and 3,096, then divide the answer by 4, and then multiply by 6, what would you get?

MELVIN: *The wrong answer.*

TEACHER: Are you good in arithmetic?

PUPIL: *Yes and no.*

TEACHER: What does that mean?

PUPIL: *Yes, I'm no good in arithmetic.*

A family of bears feeding in Yellowstone Park looked up as a car crammed with eight tourists pulled up to the side of the road.

"It's cruel," Papa Bear said to his family, "to keep them caged up like that!"

A baby bear was born in the zoo yesterday and who do you think they sent to cover the story?

A cub reporter.

Do Smokey the Bear posters help? Of course they do! Ever since they started putting Smokey the Bear posters in the New York City subways, there hasn't been a single forest fire in Manhattan.

DIT: I know a woman who is black and blue because she puts on cold cream, face cream, wrinkle cream, vanishing cream, hand cream, and skin cream every night.
DOT: *Why would that make her black and blue?*
DIT: All night long she keeps on slipping out of bed.

CUSTOMER: And this, I suppose, is one of those hideous things you call modern art?
ART DEALER: *No, it's a mirror.*

The teacher asked the class to write a composition telling what they would do if they had a million dollars.

Every pupil except Little Audrey began to write immediately. Little Audrey sat idle, twiddling her thumbs, looking out the window.

Teacher collected the papers, and Little Audrey handed in a blank sheet.

"Why Audrey," teacher said, "everyone has written two pages or more, while you have done nothing. Why is that?"

"Well," replied Little Audrey, "that's what I would do if I had a million dollars."

Boy on hands and knees looking for something.
MAN: *What are you looking for, young man?*
BOY: I lost a dollar and I can't find it.
MAN: *Don't worry, you will. A dollar doesn't go very far these days.*

TOURIST: The flies are awfully thick around here. Don't you people ever shoo them?
LOCAL: *Nope, we just let them go barefoot.*

His teenage daughter had been on the phone for half an hour. When she finally hung up, her father said, "Usually you're on the phone for at least two hours. How come this time the conversation was so short?"

"Wrong number," the daughter replied.

CUSTOMER: Waiter, this meat is bad.
WAITER: *Who told you?*
CUSTOMER: A little swallow.

CUSTOMER: Waiter, this coffee tastes like mud.
WAITER: *Of course it does, it was freshly ground.*

TEACHER: How old were you on your last birthday?
PUPIL: *Seven.*
TEACHER: How old will you be on your next birthday?
PUPIL: *Nine.*
TEACHER: That's impossible.
PUPIL: *No it isn't, teacher. I'm eight today.*

BIFF: I heard a new joke the other day. I wonder if I told it to you?
BOFF: *Is it funny?*
BIFF: Yes.
BOFF: *Then you didn't.*

I know a lady who is so fond of arguing, she won't eat anything that agrees with her.

CUSTOMER: Waiter, I can't seem to find any oysters in this oyster soup.

WAITER: *Would you expect to find angels in angel cake?*

The U.S. Government reports that 30 million people are overweight. These, of course, are only round figures.

TEACHER: Sammy, please give me an example of a double negative.

SAMMY: *I don't know none.*

TEACHER: Correct, thank you!

A little boy came home from his first day at school.

"I'm not going back tomorrow," he said.

"Why not, dear?" his mother asked.

"Well, I can't read and I can't write, and they won't let me talk—so what's the use?"

BABY SKUNK: Can I have a chemistry set?

MAMA SKUNK: *What! And smell up the house?*

"I didn't send for a piano tuner," said the puzzled housewife.

"No," replied the piano tuner, "the people next door did."

A tourist stopped at a country gas station. While his car was being serviced, he noticed an old-timer basking in the sun with a piece of rope in his hand. The tourist walked up to the old-timer and asked, "What do you have there?"

"That's a weather gauge," the old-timer replied.

"How can you possibly tell the weather with a piece of rope?"

"It's simple," said the old-timer. "When it swings back and forth, it's windy, and when it gets wet, it's raining."

IGOR: What do you have to know to teach a dog tricks?
BORIS: *More than the dog.*

NED: What kind of dog do you have there—a pointer?
FRED: *No, a disappointer.*

FLIP: What do termites do when they want to relax?
FLOP: *They take a coffee table break.*

JUDGE: The next man who raises his voice in the court will be thrown out.
PRISONER: *Hip, hip hooray!*

MIKE: Do you have holes in your underwear?

IKE: *How insulting! Of course I don't have holes in my underwear.*

MIKE: Then how do you get your feet through?

SAM: My great-grandfather fought with Napoleon, my grandfather fought with the French, and my father fought with the Americans.

PAM: *Your folks couldn't get along with anybody, could they?*

IGOR: Did you hear the story about the man who lives on onions alone?

BORIS: *No. But any man who lives on onions ought to live alone.*

Two explorers were going through the jungle when a ferocious lion appeared in front of them.

"Keep calm," said the first explorer. "Remember what we read in that book on wild animals? If you stand absolutely still and look the lion straight in the eye, he will turn tail and run."

"Fine," said the second explorer. "You've read the book, and I've read the book, but has the lion read the book?"

TIP: Stop acting like a fool!

TOP: *I'm not acting.*

DIT: Swimming is one of the best exercises for keeping the body slim and trim.

DOT: *Did you ever see a whale?*

BOY: Doc, my rabbit is sick. I can't understand it—I don't feed him anything but hair tonic.

VETERINARIAN: *Hair tonic? That's the trouble. Don't you know you're not supposed to use that stuff on your hare?*

PATIENT: You were right, doctor, when you said you would have me on my feet and walking around in no time.
DOCTOR: *I'm glad to hear you say that. When did you start walking?*
PATIENT: Right after I sold my car to pay your bill.

PATIENT: My head is stuffed, my sinuses need draining, and my chest feels like lead. Can you help me?
DOCTOR: *You need a plumber, not a doctor.*

"My brother is so strong he tore up a pack of cards with one hand."
"That's nothing. My brother rushed out the door this morning and tore up the street."

Wise man says:

Learn from the mistakes of others, because you can't live long enough to make them all by yourself.

When everything's coming your way, you're probably in the wrong lane.

Nothing is all wrong. Even a broken clock is right twice a day.

Keep your words soft and sweet—you never know when you might have to eat them.

Show me a man who always stands on his own two feet and I'll show you a man who can't get his pants on.

Even Mason and Dixon had to draw the line somewhere.

Did you hear what the termite said when he walked into the saloon? He said, "Is the bar tender here?"

> TEACHER: Harold, if one and one makes two, and two and two makes four, how much does four and four make?
> HAROLD: *That isn't fair, teacher. You answer the easy ones yourself, and leave the hard ones for us.*

TEACHER: Why are you late, Joseph?
JOSEPH: *Because of a sign down the road.*
TEACHER: What does a sign have to do with your being late?
JOSEPH: *The sign said, "School Ahead, Go Slow!"*

> Then there was this guy who was so dumb he thought the Red Sea was parted with a sea-saw.

BIFF: Only fools are certain. Wise men hesitate.
BOFF: *Are you sure of that?*
BIFF: I'm certain.

24

Rib-Ticklers

IGOR: What happens if you don't pay your exorcist?
BORIS: *You get repossessed.*

Zeke, the owner of the local general store, was the meanest, most insulting man in town.

One day a man walked into his store with a duck under his arm. Zeke said to him: "Say, what are you doing with that pig?"

"Are you crazy!" the man replied. "Can't you see this is a duck, not a pig?"

"I wasn't talking to you," Zeke said. "I was talking to the duck."

FIRST KID: When you yawn, you're
supposed to put your hand to your
mouth.
SECOND KID: *What? And get bitten?*

PASSENGER: What good is your timetable? The trains are never on time.

CONDUCTOR: *And how would you know they were late if it wasn't for the timetable?*

A tramp knocked at the door of an inn named "George and the Dragon."

"Could you spare a poor man a bite to eat?" he asked the woman who answered the door.

"No!" she screamed, slamming the door.

A few seconds later the tramp knocked again.

The same woman answered the door.

"Could I have a bite to eat?" said the tramp.

"Get out, you good-for-nothing!" shouted the woman. "And don't you ever come back!"

After a few minutes the tramp knocked at the door again.

The woman came to the door.

"Pardon," said the tramp, "but could I have a few words with George this time?"

Two men were riding on a train for the first time. They had brought along bananas to eat on the trip. Just as they began to peel the bananas, the train entered a dark tunnel.

"Have you eaten your banana yet?" cried the first man.

"No," replied his friend.

"Well don't touch it!" warned the first man. "I took one bite and went blind."

A man walking down the street saw a delivery man struggling with a large package.

"Need any help?" said the man.

"Thanks, I could use some," replied the delivery man.

They then both grabbed an end and began to struggle with the package.

After fifteen minutes, they were both exhausted.

"I guess we'd better give up," the delivery man said. "We'll never get that package on the truck."

"*On* the truck!" the man howled. "I thought you were trying to get it *off!*"

NIT: Don't you think I have savoir-faire?
WIT: *I don't think you even have carfare.*

A city dweller came to a farm and saw a beautiful horse. He decided he had to have the animal. He bargained with the farmer and the farmer finally sold him the horse.

The city man jumped on the horse and said, "Giddyup!" The horse didn't budge.

The farmer explained, "This is a special kind of horse. He'll only move if you say, 'Praise the Lord.' To stop him, you have to say, 'Amen.'"

Keeping this in mind, the new owner yelled, "Praise the Lord!" whereupon the horse took off with great speed. Soon horse and rider were headed for a cliff. Just in time the rider remembered to say "Amen!" The horse came to a screeching halt right at the edge of the cliff.

Relieved, the rider raised his eyes to heaven and exclaimed, "Praise the Lord!"

Their little baby was very quiet. It never spoke. They were pleased while he was still a baby, but as he grew up they began to worry because he never once made any sound. Finally, when the child was eight years old and had never spoken, he suddenly said, "Pass the salt, please!"

Shocked, his father asked, "How is it that in eight years you never once spoke a word?"

"Well, up to now everything was all right."

Recipe for Elephant Stew

> 2 medium-sized elephants
>
> 2 rabbits

Cut the elephants into small pieces. Add enough water for brown gravy. Cook over fire for approximately two weeks at a high temperature. Serves approximately 2,800 people.

If more people are expected, add the two rabbits. But only if necessary, because most people don't like hare in their stew.

HORACE: Day after day the boy and his dog went to school together until at last the day came when they had to part.

MORRIS: *What happened?*

HORACE: The dog graduated.

A lady went into a pet shop to buy a bird. She saw one that interested her. "What kind of bird is that?" she asked the salesman.

"That is a crunchbird," he replied. "Let me show you what he can do."

"Crunchbird, my paper!" the man ordered. The bird flew down and in one gulp ate up the sheet of paper.

"Crunchbird, my pencil!" The crunchbird swooped down and swallowed the pencil.

"He's wonderful!" said the lady. "I'll buy him."

The lady brought the bird home. Her husband looked at the bird and wondered what kind of bird it was. He had never seen a bird quite like it before.

"That, my dear," the wife boasted, "is a crunchbird."

The husband scratched his head. "Crunchbird?" he said. "Crunchbird, my foot!"

A young lady went to a fortune teller to have her fortune told.

"I will answer two questions for you for five dollars," the fortuneteller said.

The young lady paid the fortune teller but asked, "Don't you think five dollars is a lot of money for two questions?"

"Yes it is," answered the fortune teller. "Now what's your *second* question?"

BEGGAR: Pardon me, but would you give me fifty cents for a sandwich?
PASSERBY: *I don't know. Let's see the sandwich.*

"Tough luck," said the egg in the monastery. "Out of the frying pan into the friar."

Read in the will of a miserly millionaire: ". . . and to my dear nephew Sam, whom I promised to remember in my will, 'Hi there, Sam!'"

"Want to get close to something that has a lot of money in it?"
"*Sure!*"
"Go across the street and lean against the bank."

MUTT: What's that book the orchestra leader keeps looking at?
JEFF: *That is the score.*
MUTT: Really? Who's winning?

PATIENT: I am not well, doctor.

DOCTOR: *What seems to be the trouble?*

PATIENT: I work like a horse, eat like a bird, and I'm as tired as a dog.

DOCTOR: *Sounds to me like you ought to see a veterinarian, not a doctor.*

The dog and his master were shown to their seats by the theatre usher. When the picture was over, the dog applauded loudly. As they left the theatre, the usher asked, "And did your dog enjoy the movie?"

"Very much," the dog's master replied.

"Amazing!" the usher said.

"I think so, too, especially since he didn't care for the book."

"You need glasses," the eye doctor said.

"I'm already wearing glasses," replied the patient.

"In that case," the doctor said, "I need glasses."

IGOR: Doctor, I'm worried about my brother. He thinks he's an elevator.

DOCTOR: *I'll look at him. Send him up.*

IGOR: I can't. He doesn't stop at your floor.

PATIENT: Doctor, I have a tendency to get fat in certain places. What would you recommend?

DOCTOR: *Stay out of those places!*

On a cold windy day in late spring, a snail started to climb a cherry tree. Some sparrows in a nearby oak laughed at the snail. Finally, one flew over and said, "Say, don't you know there are no cherries on this tree yet?"

The snail thought a moment and said, "But there will be by the time I get there."

When my aunt heard that a milk bath is good for the skin, she asked the milkman for ten gallons.

"Do you want it pasteurized?" the milkman asked.

"No," said my aunt, "up to my knees would be fine."

Ali Baba went up to the entrance of the cave and cried:
"Open Sesame!"
A voice called back:
"Says who?"

LEM: I went riding this morning.
CLEM: *Horseback?*
LEM: Oh, sure. He got back two hours before I did.

WAITER: *Hawaii,* mister. You must be *Hungary?*
CUSTOMER: *Yes,* Siam. *But I can't* Rumania *here for long.*
Venice *dinner being served?*
WAITER: I'll *Russia* everything. What will you have? *Turkey*
fried in *Greece?*
CUSTOMER: *Whatever is ready. But can't* Jamaica *cook do it*
fast?
WAITER: *Odessa* laugh, *Juneau.* But *Alaska.*
CUSTOMER: *In the meantime I'll have a cup of* Java *with a*
Cuba *sugar.*
WAITER: Don't be *Sicily. Sweden* it yourself. I'm only here to
Serbia.
CUSTOMER: Denmark *up my check. I don't* Bolivia *know who*
I am.
WAITER: I don't *Kenya* and I don't *Caribbean* about you!
CUSTOMER: Samoa *wisecracks. What's got* India! *Do you*
think this arguing Alps *business?*
WAITER: You're a big *Spain* in the neck. *Abyssinia!*

A man was taking a walk down a street when he was stopped by someone who wanted to sell a talking dog for ten dollars.

The man could not believe his ears when the dog said, "Please buy me. My owner is a mean man. He never pets me, doesn't feed me, beats me all the time. And you know, I'm a really great dog. I also was in the last war. I won the Distinguished Service Cross and the Purple Heart."

The man was amazed. "That dog really does talk. Why in the world would you want to sell him for only ten dollars?"

The owner of the dog replied, "Because I can't stand a liar."

It was the first day of school and the pupils were very excited. The school principal visited some classes and was annoyed at the commotion made by one class in particular. Unable to bear it any longer, he opened the door and burst in. He saw one boy taller than the rest who seemed to be making the most noise. He seized the lad, dragged him into the hall, and told him to stay there until he was excused.

The principal then returned to the classroom and restored order. He lectured the class for a half an hour on the importance of good behavior. He then asked, "Any questions?"

One girl timidly stood up and said, "Please, sir, may we have our teacher back?"

A chemist stepped up to the pharmacy counter and asked for some prepared acetylsalicylic acid.

"You mean aspirin?" asked the druggist.

"Oh yes," answered the chemist. "I can never remember that name."

DRIP: After I learned the Indian dances the members of the tribe gave me an Indian name.

DROP: *What was that?*

DRIP: "Clumsy."

Fiction Best Seller List

1. *Over the Cliff* by Hugo Furst
2. *Will He or Won't He?* by Mae B. Sew
3. *Peek-A-Boo* by I.C. Hugh
4. *Who Killed Cock Robin?* by Howard I. Know
5. *High and Dry* by Rufus Leeking
6. *Early One Morning* by R. U. Upjohn
7. *Round the Mountain* by Sheila B. Cumming
8. *Is It Love?* by Midas Welby
9. *Ten Years in the Monkey House* by Bab Boone
10. *Detective Stories* by Watts E. Dunn

Non-Fiction Best Seller List

1. *I Was a Streaker* by Running Bear
2. *How to Overcome Depression* by M. I. Blue
3. *How to Avoid Arguments* by Xavier Breth
4. *Button Collecting* by Zipporah Broaken
5. *Why You Need Insurance* by Justin Case
6. *How to Improve Your Looks* by Celeste Chance
7. *Better Target Shooting* by Mr. Completely
8. *How I Struck It Rich* by Jack Potts
9. *How to Fall Out the Window* by Eileen Dover
10. *The Victims of Jack the Ripper* by Hugh Next

FIRST SHARK: Do you know what that funny-looking thing is with two legs swimming in the water?
SECOND SHARK: *No, but I'll bite.*

Astronauts Harry and Larry were on a space ship circling above the earth. According to plans, Harry would leave the space ship to go on a fifteen-minute space walk, while Larry remained inside.

When Harry tried to get back into the space ship, he found the door was locked. He knocked. There was no answer. He knocked louder. Still no answer. He pounded with all his might. Finally, he heard Larry's voice inside the space ship, "Who's there?"

GERMAN BOY: Tell me, what's your telephone number?
GERMAN GIRL: *9999999.*
GERMAN BOY: All right, then don't!

FATHER BEAR: Someone's been eating my porridge.
MOTHER BEAR: *Someone's been eating my porridge.*
BABY BEAR: Someone's been eating my porridge, and it's all gone!
GRANDMA BEAR: *I wish you'd all stop complaining. I haven't even served the porridge yet.*

"Open wide," said the dentist. "Good grief! You've got the biggest cavity I've ever seen, *the biggest cavity I've ever seen*!"

"You don't have to repeat yourself," snapped the patient.

"I didn't," said the dentist. "That was an echo."

WORSE VERSE

25

Sad Stories

An Old Bulldog

There was an old bulldog named Caesar,
Who went for a cat just to tease her;
　　　But she spat and she spit
　　　Till the old bulldog quit.
Now when poor Caesar sees her, he flees her.

At a Bullfight

At a bullfight in sunny Madrid,
A tourist went clean off his lid.
      He made straight for the bull,
        While the crowd yelled, "The fool
Will go home on a slab!"—and he did.

Two Cats in Kilkenny

There once were two cats in Kilkenny.
Each cat thought there was one too many,
        So they scratched and they fit
        And they tore and they bit,
Till instead of two—there weren't any.

But What Can I Do?

Said a gentle old man, "I suppose
I ought not to wear my best clothes.
        But what can I do?
        I have only two,
And these are no better than those."

For Richer or Poorer

There was a young man from Angora
Who married—for richer or poorer.
        He'd not been long wed,
        When he fell out of bed,
And said, "Drat, I have married a snorer!"

Died of the Shock

Here lies a young salesman named Phipps,
Who married on one of his trips
        A widow named Block.
        He died of the shock
When he saw there were six little chips.

Poor Ben

There was an old puzzler, Ben Ross,
Who died—doing crosswords, of course.
     He was buried, poor Ben,
     With eraser and pen
In a box six feet down, three across.

     —Sheila Anne Barry

Higher and Higher

There was a young girl in the choir
Whose voice went up higher and higher.
     It reached such a height,
     It was clear out of sight;
And they found it next day in the spire.

A Young Lady from Niger

There was a young lady from Niger,
Who smiled as she rode on a tiger.
　　　They came back from a ride
　　　With the lady inside,
And a smile on the face of the tiger.

In His Hot-Air Balloon

Said young Rex in his hot-air balloon,
"I shall see all the stars very soon."
　　　Rex was right, for he dropped,
　　　And he saw when he stopped
Three million bright stars and a moon.

Interrupted Two Girls

A painter who lived in Great Britain,
Interrupted two girls with their knittin'.
      He said with a sigh,
      "That park bench—well, er—I
Just painted it, right where you're sittin'."

Carried Politeness Too Far

There was a young girl from Bryn Mawr
Who carried politeness too far.
      "Don't look now," she said,
      With a tilt of her head,
"But someone is stealing your car!"

Paper Trousers

A thrifty young fellow of Shoreham
Made brown paper trousers and woreham.
      He looked nice and neat
      Till he bent in the street
To pick up a pin, then he toreham.

One More Crust

A greedy young actress once said,
As she gobbled down slices of bread,
      "If I eat one more crust,
      I'm sure I will bust"—
At which point her audience fled.

Famous Limericks

A Thoughtful Old Man

A thoughtful old man of Lahore,
When a subject was getting a bore,
   Would wisely arrange
   Conversation to change
By falling in fits on the floor.

As a Beauty

As a beauty I am not a star,
There are others more handsome by far;
   But my face—I don't mind it,
   For I am behind it;

It's the people in front that I jar.

Resembled a Pin

There was a young lady so thin
That she closely resembled a pin;
    Don't think that I'd creep
    To the window and peep,
I was told by a friend who looked in.

There Was An Old Man

There was an old man on whose nose
Most birds of the air could repose;
    But they all flew away
    At the close of the day,
Which relieved that old man and his nose.

—*Edward Lear*

Tut-Ankh-Amen

Tut-Ankh-Amen, best known as old Tankh,
Was a pharaoh of infinite rank;
    But his sarcophagus
    Wouldn't cause all this fuss
If his name had been Freddie or Frank.

Taught Ducklings

There was an old lady of France,
Who taught little ducklings to dance;
    When she said, "Tick-a-tack!"
    They only said, "Quack!"
Which grieved that old lady of France.

—*Edward Lear*

Well-Protected

Oh, I'm glad I'm protected from knocks,
From my necktie clear down to my socks,
And padded and bolstered
Fenced in and upholstered
With muscles to take up the shocks.

An Important Young Man

An important young man of Quebec
Had to welcome the Duchess of Teck.
So he bought for a dollar
A very high collar
To save himself washing his neck.

I'd Rather Have Fingers

I'd rather have fingers than toes;
I'd rather have ears than a nose;
        And as for my hair,
        I'm glad it's all there:
I'll be awfully sad when it goes.

A Princess of Bengal

There was a princess of Bengal,
Whose mouth was exceedingly small;
        Said she, "It would be
        More easy for me
To do without eating at all!"

A Moppsikon Floppsikon Bear

There was an old person of Ware
Who rode on the back of a bear;
        When they said, "Does it trot?"
        He said: "Certainly not,
It's a Moppsikon Floppsikon bear."

—*Edward Lear*

Funnily Dressed

There once was an old man of Brest,
Who was always funnily dressed:
        Who wore gloves on his nose,
        And a hat on his toes,
And a boot in the middle of his chest.

This Walking Around

I wish that my room had a floor;
I don't care very much for the door,
But this walking around
Without touching the ground
Is getting to be such a bore.

You Will Think It Absurd

Said the snail to the tortoise: "You may
Find it hard to believe what I say;
     You will think it absurd,
     But I give you my word,
They fined me for speeding today."

"Well, well!" said the tortoise. "Dear me,
How defective your motor must be!
     Though I speed every day
     Not a fine do I pay;
The police cannot catch me, you see!"

They Came from Oporta

There was once a man from Oporta
Who daily got shorter and shorter,
    The reason he said
    Was the hod on his head,
Which was filled with the heaviest mortar.

His sister named Lucy O'Finner
Grew constantly thinner and thinner,
    The reason was plain,
    She slept out in the rain,
And was never allowed any dinner.

        —Lewis Carroll

Help!

Next to the Duchess

I sat next to the Duchess at tea.
'Twas just as I feared it would be!
      Her rumblings abdominal
      Were simply phenomenal,
And everyone thought it was me!

Caught in a Flood

A singer they called Miss Diana
Was caught in a flood in Montana.
    She floated away,
      While her beau, so they say,
Accompanied her on the piana.

Call the Doctor!

There once was a boy of Baghdad,
An inquisitive sort of a lad,
    Who said, "I will see
    If a sting has a bee."
Call the doctor! (He found that it had.)

A Luckless Church Tenor

A luckless church tenor was Horace
Whose skin was so terribly porous,
    Sometimes in the choir
    He'd start to perspire,
And nearly drown out the whole chorus.

Never Look Down

There was a young girl from Mobile,
Who went up in a great Ferris Wheel.
    When halfway around,
    She looked down at the ground;
And it cost her a five-dollar meal.

A Puppy

A puppy whose hair was so flowing
There really was no way of knowing
  Which end was his head,
  Once stopped me and said,
"Please, sir, am I coming or going?"

A Bath That She Took

There once was a lady named Harris,
That nothing would ever embarrass,
  Till the powder she shook
  In the bath that she took
Turned out to be plaster of Paris.

Moans & Groans

Ex-President Taft

They say that ex-President Taft,
When hit by a golf ball, once laughed
    And said, "I'm not sore,"
    But although he called "Fore"
The place where it hit him was aft.

Slipped on a Banana

There was a young girl in Havana
Who slipped on a skin of banana.
    Away went her feet,
    And she took a seat
In a very unladylike manner.

Snored and Snored

An elephant lay in his bunk
In slumber his chest rose and sunk.
He snored and he snored,
Till the jungle folks roared—
And his wife tied a knot in his trunk.

Atlas

Despite his impressive physique,
Atlas was really quite meek.
      If a mouse showed its head,
      He would jump into bed,
With a terrible bloodcurdling shriek.

A Dentist Named Archibald Moss

A dentist named Archibald Moss
Fell in love with the dainty Miss Ross.
    But he held in abhorrence
    Her name (it was Florence),
And renamed her his Dental Floss.

Wore a Kettle

A charming old lady named Gretel,
Instead of a hat, wore a kettle.
    When they called her misguided,
    She said, "I've decided
To show all the neighbors my mettle."

A Young Lady of Cork

There was a young lady of Cork
Whose Pa made a fortune in pork.
    He bought for his daughter
    A tutor who taught her
To balance green peas on her fork.

Mamma Was a Goat

A cheese that was aged and gray
Was walking and talking one day.
    Said the cheese, "Kindly note
    My mamma was a goat
And I'm made out of curds, by the whey."

Grape Marmalade

There once was a clever young maid
Who only ate grape marmalade.
    At one hundred and three
    She said with a WHEE!
"How nicely preserved I have stayed!"

Next Page!

A newspaper reader named Gage
Would fly into a terrible rage
    When he would choose
    To read some big news
And find it continued . . .
next page!

The Gorilla's Grimace

The menagerie came to our place,
And I loved the Gorilla's grimace.
    It surprised me to learn
    That he owned the concern,
Being human, but odd in the face.

Modern Nursery Rhymes

Humpty Dumpty

Humpty Dumpty sat on a wall,
Humpty Dumpty had a great fall.
All the king's horses and all the king's men
Had scrambled eggs for breakfast again.

Jack Be Nimble

Jack be nimble, Jack be quick.
Jack, stand still; you're making me sick!

Mary Had a Little Lamb

Mary had a little lamb,
'Twas awful dumb, it's true.
It followed her in a traffic jam,
And now it's mutton stew.

Mary had a little lamb
As dirty as a hog.
They asked her how it got that way.
She answered simply, "Smog."

The Animals

Mary had a little lamb;
Freddie had a pup;
Ronnie had a crocodile.
It ate the others up.

Little Bo-Peep

Little Bo-Peep has lost her sheep
And looks for them sedately.
I hope that she will find them soon;
We've had no lamb chops lately.

Jack and Jill

Jack and Jill went up the hill
To fetch a pail of water.
Jack fell down and broke his crown
So he couldn't play king anymore.

Fleas

Some folks say that fleas are black,
But I know that's not so,
'Cause Mary had a little lamb
With fleas as white as snow.

Old Mother Hubbard

Old Mother Hubbard went to the cupboard
To get her dog a banana.
When she got there, the cupboard was bare
So the poor dog had to eat sponge cake.

Hickory, Dickory, Dock

Hickory, dickory, dock,
The mice ran up the clock,
The clock struck one;
The others escaped with minor injuries.

Still More About Mary

Mary had a little lamb,
     A lobster and some prunes,
A glass of milk, a piece of pie,
     And then some macaroons.
It made the busy waiters grin
     To see her order so,
And when they carried Mary out,
     Her face was white as snow.

Don't Spit on the Floor

When I Die

When I die, bury me deep,
Bury my history book at my feet.
Tell the teacher I've gone to rest,
And won't be back for the history test.

Message for Doctors

A doctor fell into a well
And broke his collarbone.
A doctor should attend the sick
And leave the well alone.

Gallons of Ink

There's a clever old miser who tries
Every method to e-con-o-mize.
  He says, with a wink,
  "I save gallons of ink
By simply not dotting the I's."

The Umbrella

There was a young lady of Spain,
Who couldn't go out in the rain,
  'Cause she'd lent her umbrella
  To Queen Isabella
Who never returned it again.

A Cannibal of Penzance

A cannibal bold of Penzance
Ate an uncle and two of his aunts,
  A cow and her calf,
  An ox and a half—
And now he can't button his pants.

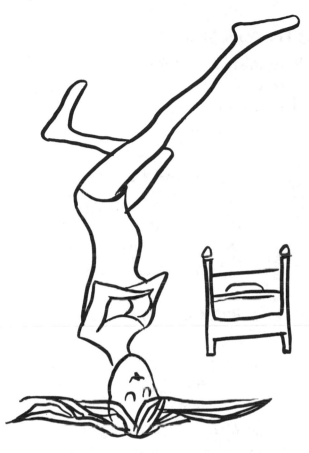

A Young Lady of Crete

There was a young lady of Crete
Who was so exceedingly neat,
    When she got out of bed,
    She stood on her head
To make sure of not soiling her feet.

I Flunked, Too

Roses are red,
Violets are blue.
I copied your paper,
And I flunked, too.

It Cooled Her Off

She wore her stockings inside out
All through the summer heat.
She said it cooled her off to turn
The hose upon her feet.

One Fine October Morning

One fine October morning
    In September, last July,
The moon lay thick upon the ground,
    The snow shone in the sky.
The flowers were singing gaily,
    And the birds were in full bloom.
I went down to the cellar
    To sweep the upstairs room.

It's Laughable

It always makes me laugh,
It's so wonderful a treat,
To see an athlete run a mile
And only move two feet.

Accident-Prone

Joe, Joe, stubbed his toe
On the way to Mexico.
In Brazil he hurt his back,
Sliding on the railroad track.
When he got home he broke a bone,
Talking on the telephone.

31

Glub Glub Glub

Every Time I Take a Bath

Giving me a washing machine
Was very nice of you,
But every time I take a bath
It beats me black and blue.

Phoebe

A certain young chap named Bill Beebee
Was in love with a lady named Phoebe.
  "But," said he, "I must see
  What the license fee be
Before Phoebe be Phoebe B. Beebee."

To the Household's Disgust

There was an old lady in Rye
Who was baked by mistake in a pie.
  To the household's disgust,
  She emerged through the crust
And exclaimed, with a yawn, "Where am I?"

Going Tomorrow

  A traveler once to his sorrow
  Requested a ticket to Morrow.
    Said the agent, "It's plain
    That there isn't a train
  To Morrow today, but tomorrow!"

A Young Lady Named Hannah

There was a young lady named Hannah
Who slipped on a peel of banana.
     She wanted to swear,
     But her mother was there,
So she whistled "The Star-Spangled Banner."

A gentleman passing (named Keller)
Picked up her brown gloves and umbrella.
     "Did you fall, ma'am?" he cried.
     "Do you think," she replied,
"I lay down for the fun of it, fella?"

A Fly and a Flea in a Flue

A fly and a flea in a flue
Were imprisoned, so what could they do?
    Said the fly, "Let us flee!"
    "Let us fly!" said the flea,
So they flew through a flaw in the flue.

A Young Lady of Lynn

    There was a young lady of Lynn
    Who was so excessively thin
That when she essayed
To drink lemonade
    She slipped through the straw and fell in.

A Young Man Called O'Toole

There was a young man called O'Toole,
Who thought he was handsome and cool.
He grew a long beard
And then, as I feared,
Tripped on it and fell in the pool.

A Phantom Named Pete

There once was a phantom named Pete,
Who never would play, drink, or eat.
He said, "I don't care
For a Coke or eclair.
Can't you see that I'm dead on my feet?"

Ezra Shank

He rocked the boat,
Did Ezra Shank.
These bubbles mark

    o

    o

    o

    o

    o

Where Ezra Sank.

As for the Bucket

There was an old man of Nantucket,
Who kept all his cash in a bucket.
      But his daughter, named Nan,
      Ran away with a man,
And as for the bucket—Nantucket.

He followed the pair to Pawtucket,
The man and the girl with the bucket,
      And he said to the man,
      "You're welcome to Nan,"
But as for the bucket—Pawtucket.

The pair tracked Paw back to Manhasset,
Where he still had the cash as an asset.
      And Nan and the man
      Stole the money and ran,
And as for the bucket—Manhasset.

32

Be Kind to the Moose

The Moose

Be kind to the moose.
He may be of use,
For hanging your hat
Or something like that . . .

Don't Worry

Don't worry if your grades are low
And your rewards are few.
Remember that the mighty oak
Was once a nut like you.

The Wizard of Oz

The fabulous Wizard of Oz
Retired from business becoz
     What with up-to-date science
     To most of his clients
He wasn't the wiz that he woz.

A Young Man of Aberdeen

A young man of fair Aberdeen
Once grew so remarkably lean,
    So flat and compressed,
      That his back touched his chest,
And sideways he couldn't be seen.

Wright Wrote

A right-handed fellow named Wright
In writing "write" always wrote "rite"
    Where he meant to write right.
    If he'd written "write" right,
Wright would not have wrought rot writing "rite."

Down the Street

Down the street his funeral goes
As sobs and wails diminish.
He died from drinking straight shellac,
But he had a lovely finish.

Which Way Did She Go?

An elephant living in Kent
Had a nose that was terribly bent.
    She followed her nose
    One day, I suppose,
And no one knows which way she went.

Our Kitten

Our kitten, the one we call Louie,
Will never eat liver so chewy,
    Nor the milk, nor the fish
    That we put in his dish.
He only will dine on chop suey.

Common Scents

The porcupine may have his quills,
The elephant his trunk;
But when it comes to common scents,
My money's on the skunk.

The Cheerful Bear

A cheerful old bear at the zoo
Could always find something to do.
When it bored him, you know,
To walk to and fro,
He reversed it and walked fro and to.

A Hunter Named Shepherd

They tell of a hunter named Shepherd
Who was eaten for lunch by a leopard.
Said the leopard, "Egad,
You'd be tastier, lad,
If you had been salted and peppered."

That's Okay

Early to bed,
Early to rise,
That's okay
For other guys.

Old Hogan's Goat

Old Hogan's goat was feeling fine,
Ate six red shirts from off the line.
Old Hogan grabbed him by the back
And tied him to the railroad track.

Now as the train came into sight,
That goat grew pale and green with fright.
He heaved a sigh as if in pain,
Coughed up those shirts and flagged the train.

The Headlight

The lightning bug is bright,
But it hasn't any mind.
It blunders on through life
With a headlight on behind.

A Dog Is Loved

A dog is loved
     By old and young.
He wags his tail
     And not his tongue.

Fuzzy Wuzzy

Fuzzy Wuzzy wuz a bear.
Fuzzy Wuzzy had no hair.
Fuzzy Wuzzy wuzn't fuzzy,
    —Wuz he?

Jokes

I'm fairly gracious to the bore
     Who tells me jokes I've heard before.
But he will find me glum and grim
     Who tells me jokes I've told to him.

GRAB
BAG

33

Best of the West

SHERIFF: How much after midnight is it?
DEPUTY: *I don't know, Sheriff. My watch only goes as high as twelve.*

How was sports equipment transported in the Old West?

By football coach.

What western city is named for a ghost?

Casper.

Who was the most famous cat in the West?

Kitty Carson.

Say These 3 Times Quickly

Six sheriffs seek six sick sheiks.

Where is the chief cheap sheep section?

What did the big buffalo say to the little
buffalo when it left for school?

"Bison!"

A Pony Express rider was attacked by a mountain lion. He rode to the nearest town and limped into the post office.

"What happened to you?" asked the postmaster.

"I was riding along when I was attacked by a mountain lion," the rider said. "Fortunately, he only bit me slightly."

"Did you put anything on your leg?"

"No, he liked it plain."

Why did Billy the Kid set Dodge City on fire?

So he could be the toast of the town.

What was Billy the Kid's favorite subject in school?

Trigonometry.

What do you call an outlaw armed with four loaded revolvers?

"Sir!"

What kind of fur do you get from outlaws?

As fur as you can get.

What kind of cat chases outlaws?

A posse cat.

Who is the thirstiest
cowboy in the West?

*The one who drank
Canada Dry.*

A cowboy visited a saloon where he saw a remarkable sight. Several cowboys were sitting around a table playing poker with a small, shaggy dog.

"What a wonderful dog," the cowboy said. "He must be very intelligent to be able to play poker with human beings."

"Not really," one of the players said. "Every time he gets a good hand, he wags his tail."

Why was the animal thrown
out of the poker game?

Because it was a cheetah.

Why were outlaws the strongest
men in the Old West?

They could hold up trains.

What do buffaloes celebrate every 200 years?

Their Bison-tennial.

34

Quick on the Draw

Say These Tongue Twisters
Three Times Quickly

A genuine judge just judges justly.

Six cattle slip on slick ski slopes.

No stagecoach stops at Smith's
fresh fish-sauce shop.

35

Mad Doctors

REPORTER: Doctor, what's the best thing to do when your ear rings?
MAD DOCTOR: *Answer it.*

REPORTER: Doctor, what's the best way to prevent diseases caused by biting insects?
MAD DOCTOR: *Don't bite any.*

NURSE: Shall we give the patient a local anesthetic, doctor?
MAD DOCTOR: *No, I'm in a hurry. Let's give him the express.*

What did the Mad Scientist get when he crossed an electric eel and a sponge?

Shock absorbers.

What did the Mad Scientist get when he crossed a cow and an elk?

A wonderful place to hang milk pails.

MAD DOCTOR: You have a condition called "Updoc."
PATIENT: *What's "Updoc?"*
MAD DOCTOR: Nothing much. What's up with you?

What did the Mad Doctor say to the patient when he finished the operation?

"That's enough out of you!"

MAD DOCTOR: The operation will cost you $400.
PATIENT: *Can't you do it for $200?*
MAD DOCTOR: Sure. But for $200, I use duller knives.

What bee is necessary to your health?
Vitamin B.

When does the Mad Doctor charge his batteries?
When he can't pay cash.

MAD DOCTOR: Please breathe out three times.
PATIENT: *Is that so you can check my lungs?*
MAD DOCTOR: No, so I can clean my eyeglasses.

What would you get if your
doctor became a vampire?
More blood tests than ever.

NURSE TO MAD DOCTOR: Doctor, you must learn not to cut so deep. This is the third table you've ruined this month.

REPORTER: Doctor, what do you talk about with the zombie that you created?
MAD DOCTOR: *Not much. I never learned to speak any dead languages.*

REPORTER: Doctor, what do you think of artificial respiration?
MAD DOCTOR: *Personally, I prefer the real thing.*

What boat takes dentists
on short trips?

The Tooth Ferry.

When does a Mad Doctor buy a thermometer?

Winter, because then it's lower.

What would you get if the Mad
Doctor swallowed a clock?

A tick doc.

MAD SCIENTIST: I saw a doctor today
about my memory.
IGOR: *What did he do?*
MAD SCIENTIST: He made me pay in
advance.

MAD SCIENTIST: Imagine you were strapped to an operating table with Dr. Frankenstein about to transplant your brain. What would you do?

IGOR: *Quit imagining!*

36

Don't Feed the Robots

Why did the Mad Scientist put a
rabbit in his automobile?

So he could use it for short hops.

When is a robot like a surgeon?

When it operates on batteries.

How does a Mad Scientist count cows?

On a cowculator.

What do you get when a robot's
wires are reversed?

A lot of backtalk.

What did the robot
say when it ran out
of electricity?

"AC come, AC go."

How do robots cross a lake?

In a row-bot.

What did the Mad Scientist get when
he crossed a cow and a chicken?

Roost beef.

What did the Mad Scientist get when he
crossed a chicken and a cement truck?

A hen that lays sidewalks.

What does a mechanical frog say?

"Robot, robot!"

How does the Mad Scientist
fix a robot gorilla?

With a monkey wrench.

What snacks should you serve robots at parties?

Assorted nuts.

What did the Mad Scientist
get when he crossed a
watch and a lollipop?

*He got a watch that
took a licking but
kept on ticking.*

What did the Mad Scientist write
on the robot's tombstone?

"RUST IN PEACE."

What did the little electric
robot say to its mother?

"I love you watts and watts."

Mad Scientist Dares You to Say These 3 Times Quickly

Will real wheels really wheel robots? If real wheels will really wheel robots, where are the robots that the real wheels really wheel?

Red leather robots, yellow leather robots.

Why did the Mad Scientist take
his robot to the psychiatrist?

Because it had a screw loose.

What kind of doctor operates
on Styrofoam robots?

A plastic surgeon.

Best Seller List

1. *Roller Coasters for Everyone* by Lupe de Lupe

2. *Astrology: What the Stars Mean* by Horace Cope

3. *Measuring School Work* by Tess D. Studenz

4. *Stunt Driving for Fun* by E. Rex Carr

5. *How to Get 100 Things Free* by Fern Otten

6. *Calming Werewolves* by Justin Casey Howells

7. *The Space Invaders* by Athena Martian

8. *Is There a Loch Ness Monster?* by Y. Knott

9. *The Big Bang Theory* by Adam Balm

10. *Reptiles Around the World* by Sally Mander

37

Zany Experiments

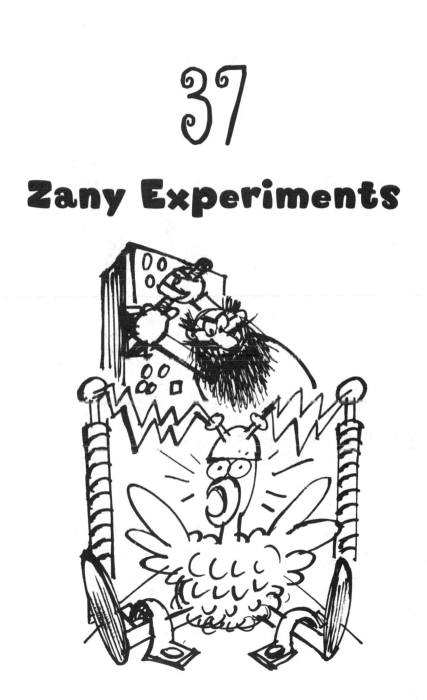

What did the Mad Scientist get when he
crossed a parrot and an army man?

A parrot-trooper.

What was the football
coach looking for in space?

An all-star team.

What did the Mad Scientist get when
he crossed a clock and a rooster?

An alarm cluck.

What did the Mad Scientist get
when he crossed a porcupine
and an alarm clock?

A stickler for punctuality.

How did the Mad Scientist make anti-freeze?

He put ice cubes in her bed.

What did the Mad Scientist get when he
crossed a banana and a banana?

A pair of slippers.

What did the Mad Scientist get when he
crossed a comedian and a spiritualist?

> *A happy medium.*

What did the Mad Scientist get when
he crossed a reindeer and a firefly?

> *Rudolph the Red-Nosed Firefly.*

What did the Mad Scientist get when
he crossed a parrot and a canary?

> *A bird who knows both the
> words and the music.*

What kind of jokes do scientists make?

Wisecracks.

What's the most educated thing in the Mad Scientist's laboratory?

A thermometer, because it has so many degrees.

Why didn't the Mad Scientist cross the Frankenstein monster with anything?

Because the Frankenstein monster doesn't like to be crossed.

Why didn't the Mad
Scientist allow the sick
eagle in his laboratory?

Because it was illegal.

What animal won't the Mad Scientist
allow in his laboratory?

A cheetah.

Why did the Mad Scientist put an
elastic band around his forehead?

So he could stretch his imagination.

What did the Mad Scientist get when
he crossed a sheep and a kangaroo?

A woolen jumper.

What goes through water but doesn't get wet?

A ray of light.

What did the Mad Scientist get when he crossed a clown and a chicken?

A comedi-hen.

What did the Mad Scientist get when he crossed a sweet potato and a jazz musician?

Yam sessions.

Best Seller List

1. *How to Live in the Swamp* by Tad Pohl

2. *Foot Problems* by Aiken Bunyan

3. *Primitive Warfare* by Beau N. Arros

4. *Polar Exploration* by R.U. Cole and I.M. Freeson

5. *How to Use Space Weapons* by Ray Gunn

6. *Getting Started in Monster-Making* by Dr. Frank N. Stein

7. *You Can Be Healthy* by Colin D. Head

8. *How to Find Zombies* by Luke Sharp

9. *Mixing Chemicals* by Yul B. Sari

10. *A Tourist's Guide to Transylvania* by Bea Ware

38

Creature Features

How do you make a strawberry shake?

Take it to a horror movie.

What do you say about a
terrible mummy movie?

"It sphinx!"

What do you call a great scary film?

A terror-ific movie.

What's dangerous, yellow, and hot?

Shark-infested custard.

What would happen if a giant sat
in front of you at the movies?

You'd miss most of the film.

Why is it good to tell ghost
stories in hot weather?

*Because they're
so chilling.*

When does a graveyard romance start?

When boy meets ghoul.

Why do dragons sleep during the day?

So they can fight knights.

Why was the werewolf hired by the radio station?

Because he had the paws for station identification.

Where do ghouls like to sit when they go to the theatre?

Dead center.

What happens to the actors when
a ghost haunts a theater?

They get stage fright.

What haunting melody do ghouls
sing early in the day?

"Oh, what a beautiful mourning . . ."

What kind of eyes does
Count Dracula admire?

Bloodshot.

Where do supernatural creatures live?

In a ghost town.

How did they ship skeletons in the Old West?

By Bony Express.

What happened to
Jesse James after a
vampire bit him?

*He became a
sick shooter.*

How does a dinosaur get
to Carnegie Hall?

By practicing his scales.

Say These 3 Times Quickly

(Heh-Heh!)

The wretched witch watched a walrus washing. Did the wretched witch watch a walrus washing? If the wretched witch watched a walrus washing, where's the washing walrus the wretched witch watched?

The ghost goes by Blue Goose bus.

Monsters chomp cheap cherry marshmallows.

The shark shops for short silk shorts.

What do you get when you cross
a werewolf with Lassie?

A pedigreed monster.

What do you get when you cross
a werewolf with a boat?

A wolf in ship's clothing.

What do you get when you cross a
werewolf with a vampire?

A fur coat that sticks close to your neck.

Who sits at the desk
in front of the class in
monster school?

The creature teacher.

IGOR: What's the plot of that new science fiction movie?
BORIS: *It's the same old story: boy meets girl, boy loses girl, boy
builds new girl.*

TV ANNOUNCER: "Because of the following
special program, the Invisible Man will not be
seen tonight."

What resembles a blob and has chrome stripes?

A deluxe blob.

How far can you walk
into a cemetery?

*Only halfway.
After that you're
walking out.*

What's the difference between a
monster and a loaf of bread?

*Well, if you don't know, remind me not
to send you out for any groceries.*

What do ghosts eat for breakfast?

Scream of Wheat.

What kind of shots do ghost
children take to prevent disease?

Boo-ster shots.

It's a lovely summer evening and Johnny and Sue are parked
on a hill overlooking town. Johnny turns to Sue and says,
"Sue, sweetheart, I have some good news and some bad
news. The good news is that at any moment we can see a
lovely full moon rise over the hill."

"Oh, you're so romantic," Sue says. "What's the bad
news?"

"I'm a werewolf! Aaargh!"

What happened to the wolf who fell
into the washing machine?

He became a wash-and-werewolf.

39

Aagh!

What doctor do you go to if you have
a sick Egyptian mummy?

> *A Cairo-practor.*

Why are mummies so nervous?

> *Because they're all wound up.*

What do you get when a giant walks
through your vegetable garden?

> *Squash.*

Why is an evil witch
like a candle?

> *They're both
> wick-ed.*

What time is it when a clock strikes 13?

It's midnight, Pacific Ghost Time.

What did the ghost have for lunch?

A boo-loney sandwich.

What magical creatures
can be found in many
lunch boxes?

Sand-witches.

What do you call monsters' cattle?

Monsteers.

What does a monster do before
he gets out of his car?

He kills the engine.

Why do skeletons catch cold
faster than other creatures?

They get chilled to the bone.

Where do monsters go when they're sick?

To a witch doctor.

What do witches enjoy for a snack on Halloween?

Hallowienies.

How does Count Dracula travel?

By blood vessel.

How can you make two vampires out of one?

*Tell it a monster joke and it will
double up with laughter.*

Sign in front of a cemetery:

**DUE TO A STRIKE, GRAVEDIGGING WILL BE
DONE BY A SKELETON CREW**

Who brings baby
Frankenstein monsters?

Frankenstorks.

SAY THESE 3 Times Quickly

(Yech!)

King Kong coops up the cute cook.

The Abominable Snowman slays
thirty-three sly, shy thrushes.

How many blocks could a blue blob break
if a blue blob could break blocks?

The skeleton shops at chop suey shops.

Sixty-six sticky skeletons.

What's the difference between
a toothache and a rainy day?

> *One is roaring with pain,*
> *the other is pouring with rain.*

GHOUL: (*to pharmacist*) I'd like some rat poison.
PHARMACIST: *Certainly. Shall I wrap it, or would you like to*
drink it here?

When vampires go to jail, where are they kept?

> *In blood cells.*

What would you get if you crossed
a dog and a vampire?

> *I don't know what you'd call it, but its*
> *bite would be worse than its bark.*

Why did the werewolf get
a job as a comedian?

> *Because he*
> *was a howl.*

40

Kooks & Spooks

What's the difference between a hungry
monster and a greedy monster?

One longs to eat, the other eats too long.

What do you call a monster
who's only three feet tall?

"Shortie."

What did King Kong say when
his sister had a baby?

"Well, I'll be a monkey's uncle!"

Who delivers baby giants?

Great big storks.

What do evil witches have for
dessert at Chinese restaurants?

Misfortune cookies.

What kind of music do mummies like?

Ragtime.

What play by Shakespeare makes monsters cry?

Romeo and Ghouliet.

What do you get if you cross a
mummy and a vampire?

A gift-wrapped bat.

Who goes to a zombie's party?

Anyone who has an engraved invitation.

Why did the vampire go
sleepwalking in its pajamas?

*It didn't have
a bat-robe.*

Say These 3 Times Quickly

(Tee-Hee)

The shiny sign says Sharks.

The Blob bit a big black and brown bear and made the big black and brown bear bleed blood badly.

The shark ate the sheep and the cheap sheep soup.

The shark shook the shipshape ship sharply.

The Blob brought a black-backed bath brush.

The Blob's big blister bled.

What do ghouls wear on
their feet in the rain?

Ghoul-oshes.

Why did Count Dracula visit the orthodontist?

For his bite.

Why does a vampire brush its teeth?

To prevent bat-breath.

What does a werewolf put on at the beach?

Moon-tan lotion.

41

Things That Go Bump in the Night

What do you call a vampire that
rides first-class in an airplane?

A passenger.

FIRST HUNTER: Did I tell you about the time I met a giant in
the woods?
SECOND HUNTER: *No, you didn't. Did you give him both*
barrels?
FIRST HUNTER: Both barrels? I gave him the whole gun!

What do werewolves call a fur coat?

"Darling."

How did the Frankenstein monster
feel about lightning?

It gave him a big charge.

When a monster
travels on an airplane,
where does he sit?

Anywhere he
wants to.

What goes "Thump, thump, thump,
swish, thump, thump, thump, swish?"

A monster wearing a wet sneaker.

What weighs 2,000 pounds and is all bone?

A skele-ton.

What slows a vampire down?

Tired blood.

MOTHER MONSTER: Don't you think Junior has a mechanical mind?

FATHER MONSTER: *He certainly does. I wish he wouldn't forget to wind it up every morning.*

What's the difference between
a kangaroo and a mummy?

One bounds around;
the other is bound around.

How did Jack defeat
the giant?

He used his bean.

What do you get if you cross
a giant with a vampire?

*A BIG pain in
the neck.*

What do you get if you cross a
vampire with a hyena?

An animal that laughs at the sight of blood.

What do you get if you cross a
vampire with a ghoul?

*I don't know. No one has ever wanted to
hang around long enough to find out.*

Why didn't the genie like
being in the bottle?

*Because it was a
jarring experience.*

What do you get if you cross a
vampire with a snowball?

Frostbite.

What do you get if you cross a jolly, fat man in a red suit with a werewolf?

Santa Claws.

What do you get if you cross a cocker spaniel, a poodle, and a ghost?

A cock-a-poodle-boo!

Two young children stood in front of a mummy case in the museum. On the bottom of the mummy case they noticed "1286 B.C."

"What does the number mean?" asked the first one.

The second one thought and said, "That must be the license of the car that hit him."

How do you get a giant out of
a box of Cracker Jacks?

Read the directions on the back of the box.

How can you tell that a giant
is under your bed?

Your nose touches the ceiling.

What happened when Count
Dracula met the pretty girl?

It was love at first bite.

What do you get if you cross a
rooster and a werewolf?

*An animal that howls when
the sun comes up.*

What do you get if you cross a
pet dog and a werewolf?

A new owner every full moon.

Why shouldn't you pull
a dinosaur by the tail?

It may only be his tail,
but it could be your
END

INDEX